With the Jewish Child in Home and Synagogue

by

Elma Ehrlich Levinger

Author of *Jewish Holyday Stories, The New Land,
Tales Old and New, In Many Lands,
The Tower of David,* etc.

NEW YORK
BLOCH PUBLISHING COMPANY
"The Jewish Book Concern"
1930

To

IDA PERLSTEIN LEVINSON

*who follows the example of her dear
mother in creating a beautiful
Jewish Home.*

FOR THE BOYS AND GIRLS WHO
READ THIS BOOK

We are going to follow the Jewish Child through the year—in his Home, his Religious School and the Synagogue. We are going to learn about many customs we ourselves have followed, and will learn their meaning. We may also discover certain ceremonies that we have not found in our own home or synagogue. For there are very many Jews in the world; some of them keep all of these customs, some only a few of them. But you Jewish children will want to know about the customs of our people, how they began, what they are like, and why they are still followed.

ELMA EHRLICH LEVINGER.

January, 1930.

CONTENTS

ILLUSTRATIONS

With the Jewish Child
in Home and Synagogue

I

WHAT WE SEE IN THE JEWISH HOME

As we enter a Jewish home we often see a sign beside the door telling us that Jews live within that house. It is a very old sign; every Jew describes it in his prayer book when he reads . . . "and thou shalt write them (the words of the Jewish Law) upon the posts of thy house and upon thy gates." (Deut. 6.)

Mezuzah

This sign is called a MEZUZAH. The word means "door-post," where this little symbol always hangs in a slanting position. In many homes it is also fastened at the door of every room. As the Mezuzah should be taken down at frequent intervals to see whether the ink has faded, we will take the Mezuzah, hanging beside the door we are about to enter, and examine it.

The case of this Mezuzah is made of olive wood from Palestine; but they are sometimes made of glass or metal. It is the inside which must always be the same. Through the small opening in the case, we see a single Hebrew word שׁדי (Shaddai, or Almighty), one of the names of God, which is written on the back of the parchment scroll the Mezuzah contains. Sometimes a Mezuzah is as long as six inches; but this one is only two inches long and the Hebrew writing on the parchment scroll is very tiny indeed. The parchment which we unroll to read is made out of the skin of a clean animal like a sheep or calf; there are certain rules for the writing of it, just as there are rules for writing the large Sefer Torah, which we

1

TOUCHING THE MEZUZAH
(*Moritz Oppenheim*)

will see later in the synagogue. For this is also a piece of sacred writing, as it contains passages from the Torah.

Let us read them together:

> "Hear O Israel, the Lord our God, the Lord is one.
> And thou shalt love the Lord, thy God, with all thy heart, with all thy soul, and with all thy might.
> And these words which I command thee this day shall be in thy heart.
> And thou shalt teach them diligently unto thy children, speaking of them when thou sittest in thy house, when thou walkest by the way, when thou liest down, and when thou risest up.
> And thou shalt bind them for a sign upon thy hand and they shall be as frontlets between thine eyes.
> And thou shalt write them upon the doorposts of thy house and upon thy gates."

This custom of having a sign beside the doorpost is a very old one; it is followed not only by Jews the world over, but also by Mohammedans. For the followers of Mohammed obey the command to keep the words of God always before them, by writing portions from their Bible, the Koran, upon their doors and windows.

The Jew, who places the Mezuzah beside his door with a prayer, obeys the commandment always to keep the words of God before him; it is also a symbol that God's blessing and protection are over his house. And old story tells that a wealthy heathen sent a pearl of great value to Rabbi Judah the Prince. In return the rabbi sent him a Mezuzah, explaining that the precious pearl would need watching, while his own humble gift would protect its owner. You will find the same thought expressed in these verses:

When I was just a little boy,
  Not more than three or four,
I asked about the wooden case
  That hung at our front door.

It was a case of olive wood,
  And held a tiny roll;
My father lifted me to see
  God's name upon the scroll.

My father said: "When great kings sleep,
  They bid their soldiers arm
And stand with swords before the door
  To guard them from all harm.

"But when a Jew has gone to bed
  Who God's commandment keeps,
This is the sign that Israel's King
  Protects him while he sleeps."

If we follow the old custom, we will place the fingers of our right hand to our lips and then touch the Mezuzah as we enter the house. The same ceremony is followed when passing the Mezuzah on the way out.

Now we are in the house. If it is a truly Jewish home, we will find a bookshelf crowded with Jewish books; there is the Bible, of course, and the Talmud; there will be a set of the *Jewish Encyclopedia*, telling you more about Jewish customs and ceremonies than we will find time for in our visits together; some Jewish histories; books of Jewish poems and stories. There are several collections of Jewish songs on top of the piano—old folk melodies, sung by the Jews during their long exile in Europe, and modern folk songs composed by the Chalutzim (pioneers) working in the fields of Palestine today. On the walls will be pictures by Jewish artists—Oppenheimer and Lilien and Pam; there may be a copy of a bas-relief done by Boris Schatz or some ornament from the Bezalel Art School he has founded at Jerusalem. All of this is very interesting, but we will turn away to the eastern wall to examine the ceremonial object which hangs there.

Mizrach

This MIZRACH is made of paper, although it may be made of cardboard or velvet. It is a picture hung upon the eastern wall toward which the Jew turns when he prays; for it is an old, old custom that the Jewish people, driven from Jerusalem so many years ago, still turn their faces toward the City of David when they pray. The Mizrach often represents scenes from the Bible, like the Sacrifice of Isaac, or Jacob's Dream. Sometimes it is engraved, sometimes p a i n t e d in bright colors, sometimes even embroidered. It may be inscribed with some verse from the Bible or the single word, Mizrach (east).

In the living room we may also find the ZEDAKAH BOX, an object once found in every Jewish home. Zedakah is the Hebrew word for righteousness, or in this case, justice. The ancient Jews had no word for charity, because they believed money given to the needy was not just being generous but a fair division of the wealth God has

Zedakah Box

sent the more fortunate. In the days when the first Temple stood, a chest with a hole in the lid was placed near the en-

trance; the worshippers dropped money into this chest to make
necessary repairs in the Temple. Later the synagogues and
Jewish schools were provided with sets of boxes, each marked
to show the purpose for which the money was collected; one
box received money for the repairs of the synagogue, one to
buy candles for the services, one to buy clothing for the poor.

The box hung in the home is generally for the collection of
money for the poor, especially of Palestine. The box we are
looking at now has a Hebrew inscription upon it which reads,
"Charity of Rabbi Meir Baal Nes." Baal Nes means the
master of miracles, for Rabbi Meir, one of the rabbis who
compiled the Talmud, is said to have performed many miracles
in his long and pious life. No man was ever more charitable
than this wise rabbi. It is told that he earned three shekels a
week; two he spent on his own household, one he gave to poor
fellow-students. Someone asked him why he did not try to
save a little for his own children. "If my children are good
the Lord will provide for them," replied Meir. "If my children are not good, they deserve nothing."

Following Rabbi Meir's example, the Jew today shares his
worldly goods with the poor. In times of joy, like a marriage
or before lighting the Sabbath candles, in times of grief like
the loss of a relative, or in moments of uncertainty, such as
departure on a long journey, the pious Jew drops a coin in the
Zedakah box. There is a beautiful prayer to be recited on this
occasion, which you may like to hear:

> "Behold I give this free gift as a charity for the poor of
> the land of Israel. O God of Meir, answer me! May it
> please Thee, O Lord, our God, and the God of our Fathers,
> as thou didst hear the prayer of Thy servant Meir, of
> blessed memory, and wast good to him, so likewise do for
> me, and for all Thy people Israel. Amen!"

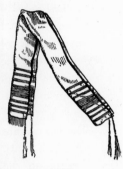

Talith

It is early morning, but the father of the family is already reciting his morning prayer. Over his shoulders father wears his praying shawl, or TALITH. The talith he wears is made of linen, although it can be made of silk or wool. Near its corners are narrow blue stripes; sometimes these stripes are black. Along the upper part, just across the neck, is a ribbon trimming called the "crown." Sometimes this "crown" is made of gold or silver embroidery. Perhaps the most important thing about the talith is its fringes at each of the four corners—silk fringes for the silk talith, linen for linen, and wool for wool. This is to follow the very old Biblical law that a Jew should not wear a garment of mixed materials. These fringes are fastened to the talith to obey the following commandment from the Book of Numbers:

> "Speak unto the children of Israel and bid them that they make them fringes in the borders of their garments, throughout their generations, and that they put upon the fringe of their borders a cord of blue; and it shall be unto you for a fringe that you may look upon it and remember all the commandments of the Lord and do them."

Because it was difficult to get the exact shade of blue for the fringes, it became customary to have them white. It is likely that in very early times the Jews fastened these fringes to the corners of the loose garments they wore all day; later, when they adopted more modern clothes, the talith became a shawl used only while at prayer. Although the father of the household we are visiting wears his talith over his shoulders, it may also be worn over the head. When he put it on, he recited this blessing, which, like so many other Jewish prayers, thanks God for the privilege of obeying His commandments:

> "Praised art Thou, O Lord our God, King of the Universe, Who has sanctified us with His commandments, and commanded us to encircle ourselves with fringes."

When the prayers are over, father will take off his talith, fold it and put it away in a beautiful silk or velvet bag, rich with embroidery. But although he no longer wears the talith gadol (large talith), he will still obey the "law of the fringes" by wearing the ARBA KANFOTH (four corners).

This garment, which is also worn by the young sons and half grown boys of the family, was put on under father's outer garments, the first thing in the morning, immediately after washing. It is really a smaller praying shawl, also made with fringes at the four corners and slipped over the wearer's head with a prayer similar to that recited while putting on the talith. The arba kanfoth is worn through-out the day. It was probably first worn,

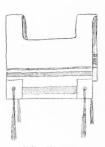

Arba Kanfoth

when Jews did not dare to wear the talith outside their garments for fear they might be recognized and persecuted by their enemies.

You will also notice that while he recites the morning prayer, father wears the phylacteries upon his forehead and left arm. Phylacteries is the Greek name commonly used today; the Hebrew term for these ceremonial objects is TEFILLIN (prayers). They are

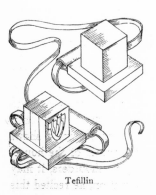

Tefillin

worn every day during the morning prayers except on the holydays and the Sabbath. Since the festivals are to remind us of our religion, the phylacteries, which are also a Jewish symbol, are not worn on these days.

When we looked over the passages written in the Mezuzah, we also read the law for the phylacteries. For in these commandments the Jew is enjoined to bind the words of God "for a sign upon thy hand, and they shall be as frontlets between thine eyes." For this reason the phylacteries are worn upon the forehead and the left hand.

Now that father has laid them aside to put them away in an embroidered velvet bag, let us examine them. They consist of long leather straps, prepared from the skin of a kosher animal and colored a deep black. There is a small box-like case on the straps worn about the arm; another box is fastened to the second strap, and, when adjusted, rests in the middle of the wearer's forehead. In this way the commandment, "a sign upon thine hand . . . frontlets between thine eyes" is obeyed. Frontlet probably refers to the ancient custom of wearing a jewel upon the forehead, the word of God being considered the most precious jewel by the Israelites.

What do these little boxes contain? The tefillin worn on the head is divided into four parts; in each part is placed a narrow strip of parchment on which is written the commandment concerning the law of wearing phylacteries. The case for the arm contains just one strip of parchment with all four passages written upon it. The strap of the head phylactery is tied behind the head into a knot having the form of the Hebrew letter daleth. On the two sides of the box appear the letter shin. The leather on the arm is wrapped so as to form the letter yod. These three letters together form the word Shaddai. I wonder how many of us remember where we last saw that word written and what it means?

The wearing of phylacteries is practised by all male ortho-dox Jews after the thirteenth year of bar mitzvah, or confirma-tion, is reached.

While we have been watching father at his prayers, we have neglected to notice the children of the household, David, who is twelve years old, and Miriam, just past nine. Their morning prayers are much shorter than their father's. No doubt many of you repeat the same words every morning yourself. David, who wears the arba kanfoth under his blouse, glances at his father's talith and is proud when he realizes that soon he will be bar mitzvah and have one to wear just like a grown man.

Now morning prayers are over and mother calls in that breakfast is ready. Although we are not half so hungry as David and Miriam, we will hurry after them, to see what hap-pens in the dining room and kitchen of many a Jewish home.

SOMETHING TO ASK YOURSELVES

1. What is the meaning of Mezuzah? Where does it hang? Describe its appearance. What does it contain?

2. What does Mizrach mean? Where is it placed and why? Describe.

3. Describe the Zedakah box. Who was Rabbi Meir?

4. What garment is worn during prayer? What is the mean-ing of the fringes? What ceremonial garment is worn all day by both Jewish men and boys?

5. Describe the phylacteries. Why are they called tefillin? What words are written on the parchment these little boxes contain, and where have we read them before?

SOMETHING TO DO

1. Bring to class one of the ceremonial objects of which you have just read and examine it for yourselves. Try to find out something especially interesting about each one—where did the olive wood case of the mezuzah come from, where were the phylacteries made, and so on.

2. Bring as many pictures as you can find of Jews using or making these ceremonial objects. You may have seen a copy of "The Scribe," painted by the famous Dutch painter, Joseph Israels; or the bridegroom wearing the talith in Rembrandt's picture of a Jewish wedding.

3. Try to find a story about one of these ceremonial objects; Zangwill has one about a talith in one of the early chapters of his most interesting book, *Children of the Ghetto*. Or bring a poem to read aloud in class.

SOMETHING TO READ

1. Translations of the Jewish prayers are found in any traditional prayer book. You have already read several of these, but it is worth while to know them all.

2. Jessie E. Sampter in *Around the Year in Rhymes* has translated some of these prayers into poetry. You will read one in the next chapter. Some of Miss Sampter's poetry describes the ceremonies you will read about in this book. You have already learned all about this one:

> They bind a sign upon the hand
> To make it heed the Lord's command,
> And 'twixt their eyes the frontlet bind
> That they may keep the Law in mind:—
> On Israel's heart and soul and will
> There stands a sign more holy still.

3. You will find another poem about one of these ceremonies we have just studied in *Poems for Young Judeans*. It is by Alter Brody. He calls it "Morning Prayer." Right after it comes "The Prayer," by Shulamith Ish Kishor, who has written many verses for Jewish children. This book is filled with poems you will want to read to your classmates.

4. In *A Book of Jewish Thoughts* (Hertz) you will find several worth-while selections on pages 191, 192. And you should like "Tephillin" by Aaron Schaffer, in Philip M. Raskin's *Anthology of Modern Jewish Poetry*.

II

A JEWISH FAMILY AT BREAKFAST

Before father and David sit down at the breakfast table, they wash their hands. Like so many of the Jewish laws this is a simple rule of health; today all of us know from our physiology lessons how dangerous it is to touch food before our hands are perfectly clean. But long ago the ancient Jew not only discovered this rule of health, but he also made it a religious ceremony. When washing the hands before meals a benediction is recited.

Jessie E. Sampter has made a free translation of this blessing:

> Blessed art thou, O God our King,
> The Lord of life and everything,
> Who made us holy with commands,
> And charged us that we wash our hands.
> (Before we eat, before we pray,
> And everywhere and every day,
> That he who with his maker stands
> Be pure of heart and clean of hands.)

Now that father is seated in his large chair at the head of the table he is ready to make MOTZE. This blessing for the beginning of the meal comes from the Hebrew word, motze (brings forth) which we find in the following benediction:

> "Blessed art Thou, O Lord our God, King of the world, Who brings forth (makes to come) bread from the earth."

Again, let us read a translation and comment by Miss Sampter:

12

Blessed art thou, O Lord our God,
King of the world, who from the clod
Makest our daily bread to grow.
(Not only we His blessing know,
But all the ripening summer days
The wheat and barley sing His praise.)

There are other blessings for other kinds of food. Before eating fruit there is a prayer of gratitude for "the fruit of the tree." There are prayers for vegetables, for foods in general, for water, and the prayer to be said over wine, which you may have heard recited on Friday evenings:

"Blessed be God, King of the world, Who created the fruit of the vine."

Now the meal begins. Father pours some cream into his coffee, and David and his sister, like all good children, empty a big pitcher of milk. There are also cream for the cereal and butter for the toast. So the family enjoy what is known as a MILCHIG (milk) meal. This is a meal where only dairy products like milk and butter and cheese may be served. Dinner will be a FLEISHIGE (flesh) meal, with pot roast, perhaps, and the usual potatoes and vegetables. Then father will drink his coffee black and the children will not have any milk; while the dessert is likely to be fruit or a pudding made without milk or butter.

The law that forbids the mixing of flesh and milk products goes back to the beginnings of Jewish history. In the book of Deuteronomy we read: "Thou shalt not seethe (cook) a kid in its mother's milk." Some scholars believe that the Jews, when they lived in the midst of the heathen nations of Canaan, were given this law that they might not be tempted to follow the pagan practise of offering up sacrifices prepared in this way. The later Jewish teachers went a step further; they not only forbade the cooking of such foods together, but said they must not be eaten at the same meal.

A still later rule declared that a vessel used for the cooking of meat could not be used for milk; that a knife which cut the butter should not be employed in slicing meat, and so on. That is why when we follow mother out into the kitchen we will find upon two separate shelves two sets of dishes so different that even a little girl like Miriam will never mix them; the dishes used for meat are painted with bright yellow flowers; the milk dishes are decorated with a broad blue band. In the same way the pots and pans and other cooking utensils are very different and are stowed away in different parts of the kitchen cupboard.

If we were invited to stay for dinner—which isn't very likely—we would learn that the delicious pot roast is KOSHER. No doubt you have often seen the letters כשר on the windows of a Jewish butcher shop. Kosher does not mean merely clean. Every good cook tries to serve only clean, wholesome food. But kosher means that the food must be prepared according to Jewish law; that it must be ritually fit for Jews to eat. The term TREFA means that the food is considered unfit for Jews to eat. Some scholars think that these laws of clean and unclean food go back to the days when the priests of some nations like the Egyptians were forbidden to eat certain food. But the Jews considered themselves "a nation of priests and a holy people"; so not only the priests among them but every Jew was called to observe the same dietary laws.

If you are interested in just what animals were permitted and what were forbidden, open your Bibles to Chapter 14 of the Book of Deuteronomy and read the list for yourselves. Briefly, a clean animal divides the hoof and chews the cud like the cow; but the unclean animal is one like the pig; although it divides the hoof it does not chew the cud.

Next, this clean animal must be butchered according to Jewish laws of SH'ECHITA (slaughter). The butcher, of course, will be a Jew who has learned all the Jewish laws which govern the slaughter of animals. He is called a SHOCHET; he must pass an examination to show that he has learned these laws thoroughly; he must be very careful not only to use just the right knife for slaughtering, but to see that the instrument is without roughness or nicks of any kind in order to kill with one stroke. When you realize how in the case of a beef, for example, it is a much quicker death for the animal than being half-stunned, you will understand why many animal-lovers, even if they are not Jews, are in favor of shechita.

Next, the shochet must examine the slaughtered animal for any blemishes that according to the Jewish dietary laws make it unfit for food. The lungs, heart, and so on must not show the slightest signs of disease. If the shochet approves, the animal is declared fit for the market; it is then stamped kosher and put on sale.

But even kosher meat needs special preparation if the Jewish dietary laws are observed. In the twelfth chapter of Deuteronomy, the ancient Hebrews were forbidden to eat of blood in any form; all animal food was to be drained to the last drop of blood before a Jew might taste of it. Perhaps in those far-off days when meat was seldom eaten except at a sacrificial feast this rite was performed by a priest; today the mother, as priestess of the home, may still follow the same law. To kosher the meat she places it in a dish which is used for no other purpose; it is soaked in cold water for half an hour; it is then thoroughly salted, allowed to drain for an hour, and finally washed in cold, running water.

There are other rules for the preparation of meat which we do not have time to study here. But there is one duty the mother performs in her kitchen that we must not forget to mention. Whenever she bakes bread, she observes the very old custom of taking the CHALLAH-PORTION. You may know that in the days when the Jewish people were all farmers and shepherds, every Jew gave a tithe, or a tenth of the products of his fields to support the priests, who, because they served in the Temple, could not plant and reap for themselves. In memory of this, the Jewish housewife takes from the mass of dough she kneads a bit about the size of an egg. After a short blessing, this bit of dough, the Challah-portion, is thrown into the fire, or allowed to bake in the oven until it is thoroughly burned, like an ancient sacrifice.

But mother will not do any baking today. For several of the neighbors are giving parties and she must get ready to attend them. Perhaps if we help her wash the breakfast dishes, being sure to put them all back on the right shelf, she will take us along! Anyhow we will read about the parties in the next chapter!

***

SOMETHING TO ASK YOURSELF

1. What two blessings begin every meal? Is this second blessing always the same?

2. What do the terms, milchig and fleishig, mean, and when did the laws concerning these foods begin?

3. If you have read the fourteenth chapter of Deuteronomy, you will be able to give a list of the animals which the Jews were allowed to use for food. Which were forbidden and why?

4. What is the meaning of shochet? What are his duties?

5. If you are a girl—boys don't have to worry about this! —tell how the Jewish housewife koshers meat for the family table. Also why and how she separates the Challah-portion?

SOMETHING TO DO

1. Again the boys who like to eat, but aren't interested in how the food is prepared, won't do **anything**! But the girls

may be anxious to describe different methods they have seen of separating the milchig and fleishig dishes and cooking utensils. Or they may want to bring to class a list of typically Jewish foods like gefillte fish, which their mothers may give them. You will be surprised to find out how Jewish cooking differs in the various countries in which the Jews have lived during their long wanderings; borsht, for one thing, is a typically Russian dish; Jews who have learned to cook in Turkey have learned to prepare fish in a special way, and so on. But do not talk about special foods for the holidays! We don't want to tell everything we know in one lesson.

2. Somebody may want to prepare a paper on the grain offerings to the Temple, suggested by the custom of the Challah-portion.

SOMETHING TO READ

1. You older readers, say those boys and girls of high school age, might enjoy reading about Jewish family meals and special feasts. There is a most interesting account in *Jewish Life in the Middle Ages* by the great Jewish scholar and writer, Israel Abrahams (especially Chapter 8). Another great Jewish scholar, Solomon Schechter, has given us a description of a Jewish meal in earlier days. Suppose you ask your teacher to read you a little of his chapter, A Glimpse of the Social Life of the Jews in the age of Jesus the Son of Sirach. She will find it on page 84 in *Studies in Judaism*, Second Series.

2. As this is really a "food chapter," you may want to read for yourselves two little Jewish stories about food. You will find them in Jack Myers, *The Story of the Jewish People*, Vol. 1: a cheese and eggs story, page 68, and the story of the date tree, page 70.

3. In this chapter you have already learned that one of the purposes of the Jewish method of slaughtering meat is to spare the animal all possible pain. In *The Jewish Library* (edited by Leo Jung) you will find a most interesting essay on this subject by Joseph Hurewitz, called "The Care of Animals in Jewish Life and Lore." Or look through the books of Leviticus and Deuteronomy in your Bibles and see how many laws you can find for the protection of dumb beasts.

III

THT JEWISH CHILD'S FIRST PARTY

Mother sets out for a party today which is given by a very young person, indeed. The child who is giving the party is a little boy just eight days old. The party is called a BRITH MILAH (from two Hebrew words meaning covenant, and cutting away). This ceremony, which is usually called the Brith, is said to go back to the days of Abraham. In the seventeenth chapter of Genesis we read how God spoke to the father of the Hebrew people: "And my covenant shall be on your flesh for an everlasting covenant." Now a covenant is a contract or agreement; among Jews, even today, the practise of circumcision recalls the old contract described in the book of Genesis, when Abraham received the rite, and promised that he and his children and his children's children would always be true to the God whom they had found in Canaan. This rite of circumcision is the first of the two great covenants which bind God and Israel; the second is observing the Sabbath. (Exodus XXXI: 13-17.)

The operation is performed by a MOHEL (circumcizer) who repeats the rite as it has been carried out for thousands of years. He must be a man who is learned in Hebrew, too, for he repeats several long and beautiful prayers; we will hear one of these benedictions in a moment.

After the mohel, the most important person at the circumcision is the SANDEK. This word, which is not Hebrew but Greek, means godfather. Perhaps some of your Christian friends have spoken of their godfathers or godmothers to you; for Christian parents at the christening of their babies select

18

two friends who promise to help the child keep his religion when he grows up. At a circumcision the sandek holds the child while the operation is being performed.

But there is somebody else who is welcomed at every circumcision although no one ever sees him. Before the operation the baby is placed upon a chair which represents the throne of Elijah and the mohel recites a prayer which begins: "This is the throne of Elijah—may he be remembered for good. For thy salvation, O Lord, I have waited." When the prayer is over the company answers: "Let us be satisfied with the goodness of Thy house, Thy holy temple."

Elijah, by the way, may be said to be the special guardian of the Jewish people. It is believed by many that he is the messenger who will some day come to announce the Messiah, Redeemer of Israel. He is also the angel of the Brith which binds Israel to God. We will hear of him again when we study the celebration of the Passover.

When the circumcision is over, the father of the child recites: "Praised art Thou, O Lord, our God, King of the world, Who has sanctified us with His commandments and enjoined upon us the circumcision." The company answers with the well-known good wishes for the little Jew, who has just been admitted into the religion of Israel: "As he has entered the covenant, so may he be permitted to enter the study of law (Torah), the marriage state (Chuppah), and the practise of good deeds (Mitzvoth)."

The ceremony is closed with the mohel's prayer over the wine, which is then tasted by the godfather and the baby's mother. Now a feast is given, as this is a great day for the family and their friends.

It happens that this baby who has just received the name of Benjamin is also the first-born son of his mother. So just thirty-one days after the Brith, there is another ceremony in baby Benjamin's home. It is called PIDYON HA-BEN. Like circumcision this is a very old ceremony. It is to remind us that when first-born sons of all the Egyptians were slain by the last of the Ten Plagues, the first-born sons of the Hebrews were left untouched. Among ancient peoples it was often the custom to sacrifice the first-born son to the gods; but the Jews "redeemed" or bought back the first son from sacrifice or temple service by a payment of money, which we are told in the eighteenth chapter of the book of Numbers amounted to five shekels. Even in our own day this money must be paid only to a descendant of the family of Aaron, the first high priest. For in the early days of our people it was the family of Aaron who served in the temple instead of the first born sons.

Today the father gives the descendant of Aaron's family five shekels (about $2.50 in American money) or a gift of greater value, if he desires. The descendant of the priests asks: "What do you prefer? To give me the first born of his mother, or to redeem him for five selahs, which thou art by law obliged to give?" And the father answers: "I prefer to redeem my son. Here is the value of his redemption, which I by law am obliged to give." Usually five silver dollars are given as the redemption money. At the end of the ceremony the descendant of Aaron places his hands upon the baby's head and recites a blessing, which concludes: "The Lord shall guard thee against all evil. He will guard thy life. Amen." Like the ceremony of the circumcision, this occasion is also celebrated by a feast, to which the family and intimate friends are invited.

Benjamin has a girl cousin who also was born just a month ago. There was no home celebration when she received the name that she shall bear in Israel; but her name, Sarah, was announced at the synagogue the first Sabbath after her birth, when her father received the honor of being called up to the platform at the reading of the Torah. In some families, this

is not done until the mother is able to go to the synagogue to
offer up thanks for the new-born daughter, and to take part in
a short special service.

While we are talking about naming a baby, you may want
to hear a little about Jewish names. Perhaps you already
know that at one time Jews did not have any family names
at all. Benjamin would not be called Benjamin Rothschild,
but because he was the son of Jacob would be known as
Benjamin, Son of Jacob, or Benjamin Ben Jacob. Later, to
avoid confusion, Jews adopted family names. Rothschild, for
example, comes from two German words, meaning red shield,
as the original Rothschild family in Germany had a red shield
painted upon a sign before their ghetto home. Or the name
might refer to the trade of the first of the family to bear it,
such as the German Kaufmann, or merchant. Often modern
Jewish family names are partly Hebrew like Jacobson; or we
have Katz and Kahn, which are derived from Cohen, the
Hebrew word for the priestly tribe of Cohanim.

But our two new friends, the babies, Benjamin and Sarah,
if they didn't sleep so much might have time to wonder what
their first names meant. As they are Bible names, these children will be interested when they grow older to find out what
famous people in the Bible first bore these names. Like all
names they also have a special meaning; in Hebrew Benjamin
is "son of my right hand" or favorite son, and Sarah is
"princess." Both of these babies are named after members of
their family; Benjamin after his mother's favorite brother who
died last year, Sarah in honor of her dead grandmother. You
may have noticed that Jewish parents seldom name their children after the living; there is no commandment against this;
but in many parts of the world this custom has been followed
so long that Jews prefer to observe it. Sometimes a Jewish
child is given a name beginning with just the initial of the

name of the relative his parents wish to honor; like Morris
for Moses; or Rae for Rachel. Of course, picking out a name
for a baby is a great deal of fun; and it is just as well to be
satisfied with our own names when we grow old enough to
know we have any. But some boys and girls are really foolish
enough to object to splendid, worthwhile names, first carried
by some great Jew and later by the child's own ancestor. A
boy who is ashamed of being named Isaac, or a girl who
changes Sarah to Shirley because she doesn't want her name
to sound too Jewish to her Christian friends ought to read the
early history of America and see how many names the Puritans
took from the Bible.

A great many lovely legends and fancies have grown up
about the Jewish baby. Some of the prettiest are about the
angel Sandalphon. Sometimes he is pictured as a rather terrible spirit made of fire; sometimes he is spoken of as "the
angel of prayer." But again he is known as the "Boy Angel";
then he becomes the special angel and protector of children.
In their games, Jewish children used to call upon him with
this quaint prayer: "Sandalphon, lord of the forest, protect
us from pain."

Even before the child is born, legend tells us that two angels
teach him the whole Jewish Law. But it would be a sad
thing if a Jewish child were born, knowing the entire Torah;
he would then be denied the joy of gathering knowledge. So
just before the baby's birth an angel strikes him upon the lip—
and he forgets everything he has learned. That is why, goes
on the story, that a baby is born crying from the blow he has
just received. You don't need to believe this; but if you look
into the mirror you can see for yourself the blow the angel
gave you before you were born; for it left a dent just above
the middle of your upper lip!

Of course, modern Jewish parents do not believe the old

superstitions about Lilith, but they are interesting just the same. Lilith was supposed to be a very unpleasant demon-lady, the first wife of Adam. She had no children; when Adam and Eve had children, she tried to hurt their little sons. She has been jealous of the babies of their descendants and might do them harm; so in olden days amulets or charms were hung about the room where the new-born baby slept to keep Lilith from making any trouble. As she was especially hateful to boy babies, another way to protect the little fellow was to have school boys come to see him and recite the Shema and some-times the ninety-first Psalm. We know that there was no Lilith to frighten away; but it must have pleased the mother to listen to the little scholars and to plan for the time when her own child would be old enough to know "the holy tongue."

You may be sure the mother thought of her young son's Hebrew education while he was still in the cradle. Even if she does not carry him to the House of Study to hear the wise rabbis lecture, as the mother of the great Rabbi Joshua did centuries ago, she still may have the same hopes for him. Many a great Jewish scholar of our own day was sung to sleep by this best-known of all Jewish lullabies:

> O! hush thee, my darling, sleep soundly, my son,
> Sleep soundly and sweetly till day has begun;
> For under the bed of good children at night
> There lies, till the morning, a kid snowy white.
> We'll send it to market to buy Sechora, (wares)
> While my little lad goes to study Torah.
> Sleep soundly at night and learn Torah by day,
> Then thou'lt be a Rabbi when I have grown gray.
> But I'll give thee to-morrow ripe nuts and a toy,
> If thou'lt sleep as I bid thee, my own little boy.

No mother would be foolish enough to give a very young child ripe nuts as a treat; but you may be sure that she did give him some very special reward like apples or a sweetmeat when he had his first Hebrew lesson. All Jewish children have the same Hebrew sentences for their first lesson. They are taught the Shema, which will form a part of so many of their prayers, both at home and in the synagogue, as they grow older.

Not so very long ago, Jewish girls were not taught much Hebrew and were rarely sent to a Talmud Torah. So the mothers seldom knew enough Hebrew to teach their young sons very long. Sometimes the father taught them their first Hebrew lessons. It was a proud day for the entire family when the rabbi came to visit and the little son was called to recite his lesson for him. Judith Ish Kishor, a writer for Jewish children, has composed a poem about this. You may want to read a little of it here:

> I like it when the Rebbi smiles;
> His face is very kind;
> But answers to the things he asks
> Are very hard to find. . . .
> "Speak, little boy!" the Rebbi says,
> "And tell your father why
> Is aleph in Va-yik-roh small?"
> And then I really try.
> "God called to Moses when most meek
> And aleph, plain to see,
> Is written small, as a sign to us
> That the first should meekest be."
> They laugh; and then, my apple earned,
> I run out very fast.
> I give a bite to Estherke,
> And eat the red side last.

Just imagine such a little boy not only knowing his Hebrew alphabet but explaining why the letter "a" is written small! No wonder the rabbi in this picture is pleased with the little boy's knowledge of Hebrew; naturally his father and mother praise and reward him. They tell him he is old enough to go to school now, and in the next chapter we will see him leaving home on the most important day he has ever known—his first day at school.

SOMETHING TO ASK YOURSELF

1. What are the two great covenants of the Jew? When is the ceremony of circumcision performed? Who is the mohel? Who is the sandek? Who is always an honored guest at the circumcision?
2. What is the rite of "Redemption of the First Born?"
3. When does the Jewish girl receive her name?
4. What is the first prayer taught to every Jewish child?

SOMETHING TO DO

1. Read how the rite of circumcision first began. (Genesis XVII). There is also an interesting story told of the first son of Moses. (Exodus IV).
2. In the days of Judas Maccabeus, the wicked Syrian ruler, Antiochus, forbade the Jews to keep their two great covenants. Look up your Jewish history and see how they obeyed him.
3. We have mentioned Jewish coins in this chapter. If you are interested in coins look up the article in the *Jewish Encyclopedia*.
4. We have used the words *ritual* and *ceremony* so often, suppose you look them up in the dictionary. And what is the exact meaning of the Hebrew words, *Talmud Torah?*

SOMETHING TO READ

1. John Godfrey Saxe has written a very interesting poem about a rabbi who was asked to attend a strange circumcision. It is called "Ben Ammi and the Fairies" and you will find it in Kohut's *A Hebrew Anthology*.
2. Zangwill describes the ceremony of the Redemption of the First Born in *The Children of the Ghetto*. Boys and girls

over twelve will find it delightful reading. It is in Chapter IV, but I am afraid if you read this one chapter you will stop reading this book and go on reading Zangwill.

3. Do you happen to know Longfellow's poem, "Sandalphon"? It is well worth reading, and will be found in any of his collected works.

IV

THE JEWISH CHILD IN SCHOOL

It is some years since our friend David, whom we met in the first chapter, put on his Arba Kanfoth and learned his first Hebrew prayers. (How many of you remember why the Arba Kanfoth was first worn and the meaning of the fringes?) When he was six years old he started to go to Hebrew School. We will not describe the modern Talmud Torah which David and his sister Miriam attend; most of you go to Hebrew school, or at least have visited one; so you know what a Talmud Torah is like today. But I am going to ask you to step back a hundred years or so with me and fly over the ocean back to Europe. Then we will see just how David's grandfather, whose name happened to be Abba, went to CHEDER.

Now it is a great day in any child's life when he goes to school for the first time. Even you readers, who feel quite grown up, may remember how excited you were that September morning (so long ago!) when you put on your new clothes, and were extra careful about attending to your ears and teeth, and couldn't eat a bit of breakfast because you were so anxious to be at school on time. Once I knew a boy who kept this up for exactly a week. The second week it took the whole family, including the maid and sometimes a neighbor, to get him behind his desk before the tardy bell rang. His name was——but I'd better stop or I'll be telling tales out of school, which is bad enough; or out of my own family, which is worse!

But a hundred years ago the first day in Hebrew School was even more important and exciting. In those days Hebrew les-

sons were not added to the education a child received in the
grammar school, for the Cheder was the only school he ever
attended.   Everything a Jewish boy learned he learned in
Cheder; there he not only studied about Judaism but learned
how to become a good Jew.

When Abba was about four his father wrapped him in a
talith and carried him to Cheder. Cheder means room; for in
most cases the first Hebrew lessons were given in a room of
the teacher's own home. There were no shiny desks and com-
fortable seats in this school room, such as boys and girls are
used to today; no blackboards or maps or pretty pictures on
the walls. There were long hard benches for the boys to sit
on, and maybe a long desk, much too high for such a tiny
fellow as Abba. The MELAMED, as the teacher was called,
usually had his hands full keeping order in a room over-
crowded with boys of all sizes and ages, from beginners who
had to be taught their aleph-beth, to boys almost ready for
bar mitzvah. He looked cross and tired and switched a strap
as he frowned at his wriggling pupils.

But the Melamed was always very gentle with beginners. He
patted Abba's curly head and congratulated him that now he
was old and wise enough to study Hebrew. That Abba might
really know "the sweetness of the Torah," the Melamed gave
him a slate on which some Hebrew letters were written. The
slate was smeared with honey, and Abba after repeating the letters as his teacher named them, didn't have to be told twice to
lick the honey off the slate as his reward. Sometimes the boy
was also given a sweet cake that he might enjoy his first
lesson. Miss Sampter has described this old custom:

> When first, a little boy of three,
> I stood beside the rabbi's knee;
> He gave me cake to make me see
> The sweetness of the Holy Book.

"More sweet than honey-comb," he said
"When once the word of God you've read,
You'll gladly live on crusts of bread
That you may know the Holy Book."

Isn't this a beautiful way to picture how our people, often persecuted and driven, cold and hungry, forgot their dangers and their troubles and their wants, as they bent over their holy books?

Later when little Abba is able to read Hebrew well, while father and mother and sister listen proudly to every word, he enjoys another treat. This is how the Hebrew poet, Jacob Cohen, pictures it:

" . . . all at once a penny drops,
Which, rolling on the table, stops.
Cries mother, 'This an angel threw—
For diligence rewarding you!'
While fear and pleasure in him join,
The timid lad takes up the coin;
He seeks the angel through the pane,
Through door and ceiling—all in vain.
(And all the others know full well
The angel's name, but they won't tell!)
The lad looks 'round and all behind him:
The angel's gone—he cannot find him!"

Let us hope that the "angel" came often to Abba's house and never forgot to drop a penny whenever he had a good lesson. But now let us come back to America and visit David's home again, because he is very anxious for us to attend his bar mitzvah party.

Although the ceremony of BAR MITZVAH is not so old as many of the ceremonies we have studied so far, it has been practised a long time. You will notice how old-fashioned the people are dressed in Oppenheim's well-known picture of a bar mitzvah gathering; though they must have considered

themselves dressed in the very latest styles. In Bible days the
Jewish boy was not considered a man, with a man's rights and
duties, until he was twenty; but later the Jews declared a boy
a mature citizen at thirteen. He was then bar mitzvah (son
of the Law) ; this meant that he could be counted in a MINYAN,
a group of ten Jews, which is the smallest number allowed
to meet for public prayer and other ceremonies. He might
be called up for the reading of the Torah; was expected to lay
tefillin, fast all days instead of a portion of the fast days,
and so on. Most important of all, the bar mitzvah was to be
held responsible for his own actions; by thirteen he knew the
laws of his fathers and was considered sensible enough to
know when he was disobeying them.

At the B'rith Milah, the boy is accepted into the Jewish com-
munity; but his parents must speak for him; it is only because
of their devotion to Judaism that he is considered one of the
great family of Israel. But at thirteen he is able to understand what Judaism means; he has been studying the history
and religion of his people; he knows what it means to be a
Jew. Now that David has reached his thirteenth birthday, the
nearest Sabbath is selected for the bar mitzvah. In the synagogue he is honored by being called up to read the prophetic
portion of the Bible, assigned to that Sabbath. For the first
time he wears a large talith like his father's, and is considered
a grown-up member of the congregation. This makes him feel
very proud; his parents are even prouder when he reads his
portion without a single error, and in a short oration thanks
them and his teachers for their loving care and instruction.

All of David's uncles and cousins and aunts come to his bar
mitzvah. There are plenty of good things to eat; congratu-
lations and presents for the new son of the Law. Everybody
pays so much attention to David that his sister Miriam would
very likely be jealous; but she comforts herself with the

thought that in a year she will graduate from Hebrew School. Then she will recite a short essay in Hebrew; there will be Hebrew songs and a Hebrew play in which she hopes to take part. With a party and presents afterwards! So Miriam is willing to have David enjoy his bar mitzvah pleasures while they last.

CONFIRMATION, which with some Jews takes the place of bar mitzvah and graduation from Hebrew School, includes both boys and girls. It is usually held at Shabuoth, the festival of the giving of the Law to Israel; this day is considered most appropriate for young Jews and Jewesses to promise to follow the religion of their fathers. The confirmants read some portion of the Torah or recite appropriate passages; some of them deliver original essays similar to the bar mitzvah oration.

SOMETHING TO ASK YOURSELVES

1. Describe the first day in a European Cheder.
2. What is the meaning of bar mitzvah? What Jewish rights and privileges has a boy who has become bar mitzvah?
3. How does confirmation differ from bar mitzvah? When and where did it begin?

SOMETHING TO DO

1. Write a composition describing your first day in Sabbath or Hebrew School.
2. Bring pictures to class showing Jewish school boys of your grandfather's time, such as The Rabbi's Visit or The First Lesson. You will find them in copies of a paper for children like *Young Judean* or *Young Israel*. In these papers, and in any of the little books, *Poems for Young Judeans,* you will be able to find verses on the Cheder, study of the Talmud, and so on.
3. Find out everything you can about Jewish education in America when there were no public schools. You will find a

good deal of information in Ch. 10, Sec. II, *History of the Jews in the United States* (Lee J. Levinger).

4. Read in the *Jewish Encyclopedia* about the two Jewish women who did a great deal for Jewish education in America —Penina Moise and Rebecca Gratz. I have a story about Miss Gratz in my volume, *The New Land*. It is called, "The Princess of Philadelphia."

5. Get somebody who knows Jewish music to sing you the old Cheder song, "Off'n Pripichick."

SOMETHING TO READ

1. You have seen how little Abba first learned his Aleph-Beth, or, as we would say in English, his A B C's. There is a fine legend about the Hebrew alphabet in *The Heaven on the Sea*, a collection of Jewish stories by Sulamith Ish Kishor. A. S. Isaacs also has some alphabet stories in his book, *Under the Sabbath Lamp*" (p. 201, p. 257-9).

2. The most interesting stories I ever read of a Jewish school boy were in *Idylls of the Gass* by Martha Wolfenstein. Just begin to read them and see whether you agree with me!

3. Sholem Aleichem, one of the greatest of Yiddish writers, has described life in a European Cheder in "Boaz the Teacher" and "A Lost Lag Ba'omer." These stories have been translated in a book called *Jewish Children*. Also read pages 31-34 in Mary Antin's *The Promised Land*. There is a description of the old-time Cheder in *The Story of the Jew* (Levinger), Ch. X, part 6. You will find an account of Jewish education in America today in *History of the Jews in the United States* (Levinger) Chapter XXV.

4. Of course, we cannot leave out Israel Zangwill! In *Children of the Ghetto*, Ch. XIII, he has written a delightful account of a bar mitzvah party. And if you want to read a sad story of a bar mitzvah, that wasn't a bar mitzvah at all, turn to the tale of the blind boy, first in his collection of stories called *They That Walk in Darkness*.

V

A JEWISH WEDDING AND A
JEWISH FUNERAL

Miriam was very happy. Like all girls she loved parties and pretty dresses; now, a month after her own graduation party, her Aunt Dora was married. Aunt Dora lived in Brooklyn; that meant a long trip on the train with a day at Niagara Falls, which Miriam and David had never seen before. Best of all, Aunt Dora had some last minute shopping to do, and allowed Miriam to help her. Then at the end of a week of buying gloves and shoes, excitement over the wedding cake, and packing suitcases, Miriam saw her first Jewish wedding.

Several years before Miriam had been invited to the wedding of her school teacher. Now she saw that in many ways a Jewish and other weddings are alike. But she was interested to notice that there were certain ceremonies which are only practiced at a Jewish wedding, and was glad to have her father explain them.

Like Miriam's teacher, this Jewish bride wore a long white veil, a custom which has come down from the Romans. There were bridesmaids in fluffy pink; the big hall was beautiful with flowers. But the marriage ceremony was performed under a CHUPPAH, a canopy fast-

Chuppah

ened to four poles, which were held by near relatives of the bride and groom. On a small table beside the rabbi, who performed the ceremony, stood two lighted candles and two cups of wine.

Before explaining the meaning of the Chuppah to the children, their father told them a little of the KETHUBAH, or marriage contract. He explained that years ago in Europe, when the Jewish people had their own laws and courts, they were married according to their own customs. The Kethubah, which was much more important then than nowadays, goes back to very ancient times. It was the contract which allowed the bride certain property rights and was very necessary in the days when the laws did not protect women as they do today. This is signed by the witnesses before it is delivered to the bride, and is one of the reasons why no Jewish marriage takes place on the Sabbath or holy days, when writing is forbidden.

In earlier days, when it was not considered proper for young people to pick out the persons they intended to marry, arrangements between the parents were handled by a marriage broker, called a SHADCHAN. When Jewish groups were small and far apart, and travel was dangerous and difficult, the shadchan was necessary to bring people together; he also took a hand in settling the dowry, and so on. Another old custom, which has almost entirely died out in America, is cutting the bride's hair. In olden times, a woman's hair was cut on her wedding day, and she was never seen afterward without a kerchief upon her head or a close-fitting wig called a SHAITEL.

The Chuppah, which is made of richly embroidered cloth or a large talith, may come down from the days when a canopy, such as those carried over royal persons, was borne over the bridal pair in the wedding procession. It is also used to represent the house which the bride and groom will share together when they are married and live under one roof.

Wine is used at all Jewish feasts. Here it is served in two goblets, one representing the joys of life, one the sorrows. These two cups are shared by the bridegroom and bride, who hope to go through life sharing alike each other's pleasures and disappointments.

The wedding ring has played an important part in the marriage ceremonies of many races. At one time brides were bought from their fathers; later a single piece of money came to represent the dowry which she brought to her husband. Then a hole was cut through the coin and it became a ring. This ring is placed upon the bride's finger by the groom, with the words: "Behold, thou art consecrated unto me by means of this ring, according to the laws of Moses and Israel."

The seven blessings are pronounced by the rabbi; when they are over, the bridegroom breaks a glass. It is thought that this custom goes back to a wedding in ancient times, when the company became too merry, and the master of the feast reminded them of the misfortunes of life by breaking a valuable vase. But some of us like to believe that even in their happiest moments Jews cannot forget the sorrows that have come to our people, and break a glass in memory of shattered and conquered Jerusalem.

According to Jewish law, the most important part of the marriage ceremony is the words spoken by the bridegroom, when he places the ring upon his bride's finger and declares that he has taken her for his wife. If the necessary number of witnesses are present, this makes the marriage binding and complete, as far as the Jewish religion is concerned. In fact, a rabbi is not needed, as any Jew may be called upon to pronounce the blessings.

But as the marriage we have just witnessed is performed in

America, the laws of the United States must also be obeyed. According to the laws of this and most European countries, a marriage may be celebrated with any religious rites the bride and groom desire; but in order that the state consider it a real marriage, certain laws of the land must be obeyed. There must be a marriage license and the marriage must be performed either by an officer of the state, such as a justice of the peace, or some person who is allowed to represent the state. So at a Jewish marriage a rabbi takes the place of the state official; when he pronounces the bride and groom man and wife, he does so not only according to the laws of Israel, but also of the state in which he lives.

Miriam and David wanted to stay in the east a little while and visit New York and Philadelphia and the other cities they had read about in their histories. But the death of their grandmother, whom they had left sick at home, obliged them to return at once. Now for the first time the children attended a Jewish funeral and learned of certain customs which the Jewish people have always associated with death.

You know that the first Hebrew taught to the Jewish child is the Shema; the words "Hear, O Israel" begin the last prayer on the lips of the dying Jew. If he is too weak to speak, the prayer for the dying is recited by those about the bed. Directly after death, the mourners repeat together: "Praised be Thou, O Judge of Truth!"

Now comes the very old custom of KERIAH, or tearing. Tearing a rent in one's clothing is an oriental mourning ceremony to show that the mourner does not take any pride in his appearance. For the same reason the mirrors are covered or turned to the wall.

Jewish funerals should be very simple. At one time it was the custom to lay the dead away dressed in costly garments; then a good rabbi decided it was easier for the poor if all funerals could be inexpensive, and the poor man would not be put to shame by the extravagant burial pomp of the rich. For that reason even today there is no unnecessary expense at a Jewish funeral; the Christian custom of wearing black mourning garments and bringing flowers to decorate the grave is also forbidden. In many cases honor is paid to the dead by donating the money, which would otherwise be spent on flowers, to some charity. Perhaps you remember the Zedakah box we saw when we first entered the Jewish home; David and Miriam had dropped coins in it for their bar mitzvah and graduation and their aunt's wedding; now they honored their charitable grandmother by giving charity in her memory.

Another beautiful old custom was carried out at grandmother's funeral. For years she had kept a little bag among such treasures as her dead husband's talith and her family pictures. One day she opened it and showed the children what the little bag contained—dust of the soil of Palestine. "I have never been blessed with the sight of the land of Israel," grandmother told the children. "But I received this precious soil from my brother when he came home from the land of our fathers. I have always treasured it, and when I die, I shall sleep my last sleep with the earth of Eretz Yisroel beneath my head."

When the family returned from the BETH HAYIM (House of Life), as the cemetery is called in Hebrew, they followed the custom of "sitting SHIVAH." Shivah means seven; for seven days the closest relatives of the dead remain in the house, sitting upon the floor, as the Jews used to mourn in olden times, or more often on low stools. Among the foods which their friends bring the mourners are eggs; the shape of an egg has no beginning nor end and represents life everlasting.

Every morning and evening prayers were offered in the house of mourning, a number of more distant relatives and neighbors coming in to make up the required minyan. (Do you remember how many Jews are needed to complete a minyan?) You may be sure that David was glad he had been bar mitzvah and was old enough to join the men and be counted with them for prayer. On the Sabbath eve following the funeral the family attended services at the synagogue.

The second mourning lasts thirty days, including the first seven. For eleven months, beginning with the burial, mourners attend the synagogue every day in order to recite the KADDISH. The Kaddish, which is written in Aramaic, is one of the best known of all Jewish prayers; its name means sanctification, for it is a prayer glorifying God's great name, and in no way a prayer for the dead. It is never said in private; for it is believed that by reciting the Kaddish as a member of a Jewish congregation, the mourner honors the dead by testifying that he is following the Jewish religion as the departed taught him to do. The Kaddish is recited at every synagogue service; on Yom Kippur, Passover, Shabuoth, and Succoth a special time for a memorial service is set aside for honoring the memory of the dead.

The Kaddish is always recited on the anniversary of a death; this is called YAHRZEIT (year-time). You will notice the words are German; the custom probably began in Germany, as well as the ceremony of lighting a candle of remembrance for the anniversary. Immediately after death takes place, a light is kindled and kept burning for thirty days. The Bible speaks of the soul of man as a light; the burning flame represents the soul of man which lives on, even after the body dies. These Yahrzeit lights are also kindled for Yom Kippur.

SOMETHING TO ASK YOURSELVES

1. What will you see at a Jewish wedding that you will not see at a Christian ceremony?

2. What is the meaning of Kethubah, and for whose protection was it made?

3. Describe and give the meaning of the Chuppah. The two cups of wine.

4. What words are spoken by the groom when placing the ring on the bride's finger?

5. Why is a glass broken at a Jewish wedding?

6. Explain the difference between a religious and a civil marriage ceremony.

7. What are the first and last Hebrew words recited by the Jew?

8. What makes a Jewish funeral different from Christian burials?

9. Describe the days of mourning.

10. What is the meaning of the Kaddish? When is it recited?

Something to Do

1. If you are reading any book on another country, say like China, try to find out something about the wedding and funeral customs of the people.

2. If you know anybody from Palestine, get him to tell you about a Palestinian wedding, and bring the report to class.

3. Find the translation of the Kaddish in the prayer book; write a paraphrase of it. This means, tell in your own words the central idea o this beautiful prayer.

4. Write a story in which one of the ceremonies described in this chapter has a prominent place. What about a story of a bride who uses a very old talith, found in an unusual way, for her chuppah? Or how somebody receives a bag of earth of Palestine—or loses it?

Something to Read

1. There is a jolly story of an old time wedding, "An Original Strike," by Mordecai Spektor, which you will find translated in *Yiddish Tales*.

2. Here comes Israel Zangwill again! If you don't believe

that a wedding, according to Jewish law, can be a very simple matter, read Ch. IV in *Children of the Ghetto*.

3. Jewish poets have written a great many marriage songs. Some of the loveliest were written by Judah Halevi, and may be read in his volume of translated poems, in the Jewish Classic series.

4. Speaking of poetry—if you like it, and I hope you do!—a story of a faithful and clever Jewish wife has been told in rhyme by Sabine Baring-Gould. You may want to read it in Kohut's *A Hebrew Anthology*, Vol. I.

5. Perhaps the most famous of Jewish romances is that of Rabbi Akiba and his wife, Rachel. It has been retold by A. S. Isaacs in his *Stories from the Rabbis*. You may read it under the title, "Rachel and Akiba, the Shepherd," in *Great Men in Israel*," by J. Max Weis.

6. There is a beautiful explanation of the Kaddish on page 199 in *A Book of Jewish Thoughts;* it is written by L. Kompert.

VI

SABBATH AT HOME

It is late Friday afternoon. Mother has been busy all afternoon in the kitchen, preparing fish and chicken, and baking

Challah

the Challah; now the two twisted loaves stand at one end of the table, covered with a snowy white cloth. Miriam has been helping her mother, for there is always a great deal to do to welcome the Sabbath Bride. Miriam has set the table with one of the best tablecloths and the prettiest dishes; at one end she has placed the silver kiddush cup, filled with wine, and two heavy brass candlesticks. Miriam polishes them every week, and sees that there are fresh candles in them all ready for her mother to light in honor of Princess Sabbath.

"I guess the bad angel will be disappointed again," says Miriam as she buttons the last button of her Shabbas dress and brushes her curls.

"What do you mean by the bad angel?" asks her cousin, Alice, who is spending the Sabbath with her relatives for the first time.

"I'll tell you the story of the two angels," answers Miriam. "There's just time enough before father comes home from synagogue."

Alice, who loves stories, curls up in a big chair to listen comfortably; we may as well listen too.

On Friday afternoon when a Jew leaves the synagogue after

the Mincha service, two angels fly beside him. One is dressed
in white; her face is gentle and loving. But one is dressed in
black, with tangled hair and a cruel, ugly face. When the Jew
enters his house, both angels peep through the door over his
shoulder. If the house is untidy, and the mother and children
are not dressed to welcome the Sabbath Bride, and the table
is not set for the Sabbath meal with wine and lighted candles,
the bad angel is happy. He says, "May all this Jew's Sabbaths and week days be like this one!" Then the good angel
says sadly, "May it be so! Amen." But if the house is clean,
with everything in order, and the table is set with lighted
candles and wine, and the children and the mother are dressed
in their best, the good angel is happy, and cries: "May the
next Sabbath and all following ones be like this!" Then the
bad, trouble-loving angel is disappointed, but he is forced to
say, "Amen!"

"But you don't believe that two real angels are coming, do
you?" asked Alice, glancing toward the door.

"Mother says it's a parable," answered Miriam. "It's like
a fairy story that teaches a lesson. The story isn't exactly
true; but it is true that if you keep the Sabbath and welcome
it joyfully, it will come every week like a good angel and
bless you."

"When I was a very little boy, I learned a poem about preparing for the Sabbath," said David. (I hope you will listen
politely while he says it, for I wrote it myself!)

Sabbath Eve

My mother cleaned the house today,
　Till all was shining bright;
For Sabbath Queen is on her way,
　And she will come tonight.
Said mother: "Little son of mine,
　The house is clean and sweet;

I've blessed the candles that will shine
To guide Queen Sabbath's feet.
But, little son, have you swept clean
Your heart and set a light,
Within your soul for Sabbath Queen
When she comes here tonight?"

"Well, I don't care much for poetry," said Alice (which was rude of her!) "But what do you mean by the Queen Sabbath, and the Sabbath Queen, and Princess Sabbath?"

"It is an old name for the Sabbath Day," David told her. "Father once told Miriam and me what a hard time the Jews used to have; working hard all week, they were forced to wear a badge to show they belonged to a lower class. When they went out of the ghetto, where they were obliged to live behind locked doors, the people used to stone them and set their dogs on them. A Jew was made to feel like a slave all through the week; but on Friday night when he returned to his own house and bathed and put on clean clothes, and sat down to a fine meal. he felt like a real prince. Then he thought of the Sabbath as a lovely princess who came to visit him."

"When I went to Aunt Dora's wedding," interrupted Miriam, "she showed me some poetry written by a German Jew named Heinrich Heine. There was one about the Princess Sabbath and she translated part of it to me. I remember some of it," and Miriam repeated:

His name is Israel,
And a witch's spell has changed him
To the likeness of a dog . . .
But on every Friday evening,
On a sudden, in the twilight,
The enchantment weakens, ceases,
And the dog once more is human . . .
'Tis the wedding of Prince Israel
And the gentle Princess Sabbath.

"There is a good deal in the poem about the Shabbas Shalet," added Miriam. "Mother has made some for tonight and it tastes better than anything we have all week."

"Well, you know the old story of Rabbi Judah ha Nassi and the Roman emperor," reminded her brother. "The emperor asked the rabbi what spices he used to make his Sabbath dinner taste better than the biggest feasts given in the palace. The rabbi told him that the spice of the Sabbath made the plainest food taste better than anything else in the world. But hush, mother is going to light the Sabbath candles!"

You all know that in early days there was no electricity or gas to make houses pleasant and inviting. But on feast days or in honor of a guest, extra lamps were lighted or more candles burned. So the Sabbath Bride was always welcomed with some kind of extra lights. Perhaps you may have seen an old fashioned Sabbath lamp hung from the ceiling, or a brass candelabra. In certain parts of Europe, a candle was lighted for every member of the family. But in America the Jewish mother usually lights two candles in candlesticks which she may treasure because her own mother and grandmother once said the blessing over them every Sabbath. The mother's blessing over the lighted candles which is the first welcome to the Sabbath Princess, is spoken just before sunset and reads: "Blessed art Thou, O Lord our God, King of the world, Who hast sanctified us by Thy commandments, and commanded us to kindle the Sabbath Lights." This is usually followed by a murmured prayer, in which the mother asks God's blessing over the household for the coming week.

When three stars appear in the sky the Sabbath has really begun. The mother, as priestess of the home, has done her part; now the father, who will act as priest at the home altar, returns from the synagogue. No one has ever described this

better than Israel Zangwill in the few stanzas we will read
from his poem,

THE HEBREW'S FRIDAY NIGHT

The father from the Synagogue returns
  (A singing-bird is nestling at his heart),
And from without the festive light discerns,
    Which tells his faithful wife has done her part
    To welcome Sabbath with domestic art.
He enters and perceives the picture true,
    And tears unbidden from his eyelids start,
As Paradise thus opens on his view,

And then he smiles and thanks his God he is a Jew.
For "Friday-night" is written on his home
    In fair white characters; his wife has spread
The snowy Sabbath-cloth; the Hebrew tome,
    The flask and cup are at the table's head,
    There's Sabbath magic in the very bread,
And royal fare the humble dishes seem;
    A holy light the Sabbath candles shed;
Around his children's shining faces beam;
He feels the strife of every day a far-off dream.

His buxom wife he kisses, then he lays
    Upon each child's young head two loving hands
Of benediction, so in after-days,
    When they shall be afar in other lands,
    They shall be knit to God and home by bands
Of sacred memory. And then he makes
    The blessing o'er the wine, and while each stands,
The quaintly convoluted bread he breaks,
Which tastes to all tonight more sweet than honeyed cakes.

Perhaps some of you have seen Oppenheim's picture of
this scene—the lighted candles, the happy mother, the father
at the door blessing the two children who come to meet him.
He then greets his wife with a passage from the Bible, praising the Jewish woman and homemaker. Near him stands the

Sabbath guest. A Jew always likes to spend his Sabbath at home, but if he is in a strange city it means a great deal to be invited to a Jewish home on Friday night. In the Middle Ages, when there were few inns, and a Jew was never welcome except among his own people, Jewish travelers upon coming to a town always went first to the synagogue. Here they hoped to meet fellow Jews who would take them home for the night. The custom we find today in some congregations of blessing a cup of wine before the congregation as part of the Sabbath eve service, goes back to the cup of wine which was sanctified in the synagogue for the benefit of homeless strangers.

Kiddush Cup

Now the family and their guest are seated around the table. If you have read Zangwill's poem carefully, you will know that first the father says the blessing over the wine. This is called KIDDUSH (sanctification or blessing) and runs: "Praised art Thou O Lord our God, King of the World, who created the fruit of the vine." The wine cup is passed about the table that each person may have a sip. Then father breaks the bread and says the blessing which you have already read in an earlier chapter.

Pieces of the Challah are passed around the table as it was served in olden days. It is said that two loaves are placed upon the table on this night in remembrance of the double portion of manna given to the Israelites in the desert on Friday, that they might have enough for the Sabbath on which they were forbidden to gather it. We think that the covering of the bread may also represent the manna that covered the desert for the hungry wanderers to eat.

You may wonder why wine is used in the Sabbath service described here; later we will again mention the two cups of wine at the Jewish wedding and also the four cups drunk as part of the Passover service. You may ask, perhaps, why wine, as an ordinary drink now forbidden by the government of the United States, may be used by law-keeping Jews as part of a religious festival. The government of this country has decided that wine may be drunk at such festivals; it is also permitted in churches of other faiths.

Such wine is known as sacramental wine, wine used for a sacrament or religious ceremony. It may be bought on an order written by a minister or rabbi. So it is not against the law for Jews to use wine for such a purpose. But many Jewish leaders believe that it is better to follow the custom of the country in which we live and substitute grape juice or unfermented wine.

After the meal Princess Sabbath receives a truly royal welcome. Three hundred years ago Solomon Alkabetz wrote a Sabbath hymn named "LECHA DODI" (Come, my beloved), a greeting to the dear Sabbath Princess. This is still sung both in the home and the synagogue on Friday eve. This is one of the best known and best loved of all Hebrew songs. It begins:

> Come, my beloved, with chorusing praise,
> Welcome the Sabbath Bride, Queen of the days.
> Sabbath, to welcome thee, joyous we haste;
> Fountain of blessing from ever thou wast,
> First in God's planning, though fashioned the last—
> Crown of His handiwork, chiefest of days.

A number of other old Hebrew songs called ZEMIROTH are often sung around the family table.

Sabbath day is spent in rest and simple pleasures. In the morning the family go to the synagogue; we will see them there in our next chapter.

No work is done within the home, for the Sabbath has been ordained as a rest day. The most observant Jew will not kindle a fire on Saturday; but he is permitted to have this service performed by a non-Jew. Father remains home from business or work; mother, who has done her shopping and cooking the day before, has a real rest day, and the children are free from school. Now that he has been bar mitzvah, David goes to the synagogue in the afternoon with his father, and listens to a reading and discussion of some great Jewish work. "The Sayings of the Fathers," an old collection of wise and witty maxims, is the book oftenest read.

But now let us pretend that Sabbath is over. We have seen the Princess enter a Jewish home; let us watch her depart. The ceremony of saying goodbye to Princess Sabbath is called HABDALAH (separation), because it marks the separation of the holy day from the rest of the week which follows it. This ceremony is performed just after dark on Saturday. Again blessings are recited over the wine cup; a box filled with spices (besamim) is shaken as the Princess takes her departure. When father holds his hands over the candles in blessing, he allows the light to shine upon his finger nails; the shadows between his fingers are to represent the separation between darkness and light, between the ordinary days of the week and the Sabbath.

Besamim
Box

Some of the songs sung at the Habdalah ceremony refer to our old friend Elijah whom we have already met at the Brith. A legend says that Elijah does not appear on the eve of Sabbath, but prefers to visit his Jewish friends on Saturday

SABBATH AFTERNOON

(*Moritz Oppenheimer*)

GOOD-BYE TO PRINCESS SABBATH
(*Moritz Oppenheimer*)

evening if they have kept the Sabbath faithfully, that he may give them strength for another week of work.

Before we leave this Jewish home where we have welcomed the Sabbath Princess and helped to speed her on her way, let us read together another poem of Miss Sampter's called

HABDALAH

Blessed be He that gave us days
For work and rest, to serve and praise
In orderly and seemly ways.
That set the bounds of day and night
With fine distinctions in His sight,
And bade us honor them with light.
Blessed be He whose Sabbath rest
With song and wine and light expressed,
Shall make the days of labor blest.

SOMETHING TO ASK YOURSELVES

1. Tell the story of the two angels; what do they expect to see in a Jewish home on Friday night?

2. What is the mother's share in the Sabbath Eve ceremony?

3. How does the father greet the children on his return from the synagogue on Friday night? How does he greet the mother? Who does he often bring with him?

4. Describe the beginning of the Sabbath meal. What happens when the meal is over?

5. How is the Sabbath day observed?

6. What is the meaning of Habdalah? What is the purpose of the candles, the spices?

SOMETHING TO DO

1. Find out for yourself which of the Ten Commandments tells how the Sabbath should be kept. Also where in the Bible the first Sabbath is mentioned.

2. If you have never heard it, ask your rabbi or teacher to tell you the blessing which the father gives the children on Sabbath eve.

3. Look up in Proverbs 31:1-31 the description of the worthy woman, which is repeated to the mother of the family on Friday night. How does the life of the modern Jewish mother differ from this good woman's?

4. Compare the Zangwill poem given in this chapter to the famous poem of the Scotchman, Robert Burns, "The Cotter's Saturday Night." How are they alike? How do they differ?

5. The great Jewish writer, Achad Ha'am, has said: "Far more than, Israel has kept the Sabbath, it is the Sabbath that has kept Israel." Write a short essay on this idea, proving that it is true. (You may want to talk it over with your teacher first.)

6. If you are clever with your hands try to do one of these things: mould a Kiddush cup or candlesticks; embroider a Challah cloth to surprise your mother; make a pasteboard model of a table set for the Sabbath.

7. Write an original Sabbath story. (Of course, this means a made-up story out of your own head, not from a book. But it will be all right if you weave your plot around some well-known Sabbath legend—like that of the two angels.

8. You will find a number of Sabbath poems in any collection of Jewish poetry. Learn a poem to recite in class. Or study some Zemiroth with the director of your choir.

SOMETHING TO READ

1. Martha Wolfenstein's book, *Idylls of the Gass*, gives us a picture of how our fathers kept the Sabbath in other days.

2. "The Sabbath Pearls" and "The Pious Woodcutter" are interesting stories by Sulamith Ish Kishor in her book, *The Heaven on the Sea*. You will also enjoy "Stars and Candles," some verses in the same volume.

3. Here are some good Sabbath stories in *Kasriel the Watchman* by Rufus Learsi; "A Manna Sabbath Meal"; "The Saving Light"; "The Sabbath Guest."

4. An interesting folk tale is "Joseph the Sabbath Lover" in *The Jewish Fairy Book* by Gerald Friedlander.

5. Here are a few of my own Sabbath stories: "Judith's Candlesticks" in *Jewish Holyday Stories;* "The Guiding Stars" in *Tales Old and New;* "The River of Dreams" in *In Many Lands.*

VII

SABBATH IN THE SYNAGOGUE

We have just seen how a Jewish family observes the Sabbath at home. Before we go to the synagogue, it should be interesting to learn a little of how the Sabbath began and what it has come to mean, not only to the Jewish people but to the followers of the two daughter religions, Christianity and Mohammedanism.

Turn to the very first pages of your Bible; there in the second chapter of the book of Genesis you will find that one day of the week was set aside as holy. For here we read that after God made the earth and the heavens and the sea and all living creatures, He made holy the seventh day on which He rested from creation.

Later the people of Israel, when Moses had led them out of Egyptian slavery, were commanded to keep this holy day as a rest day. In the previous chapter you were asked to look up the commandment which tells the Israelite how he must observe his Sabbath. But did you find out that the Fourth Commandment is given in two different ways in two books of the Bible? In the Book of Exodus, the Hebrews are reminded of the divine beginning of the Sabbath day: "Remember the Sabbath day to keep it holy . . . for in six days the Lord made the heavens and the earth . . . and rested on the seventh day."

But in the Book of Deuteronomy, instead of referring to the Creation, the commandment reminds the children of Israel of a humane reason for keeping the Sabbath as a rest day: "And thou shalt remember that thou wast a slave in the land of

Egypt, and the Lord thy God brought thee out thence by a mighty hand and by an outstretched arm; therefore the Lord thy God commanded thee to keep the Sabbath day." So here the Jew is commanded to keep the Sabbath not only for his own sake, but for the sake of his servants, and, as you know if you have read the whole commandment, even the dumb beasts that labor for him through the week.

So the Sabbath is observed to remember God both as the Creator of the world and as the Protector of the Jewish people; it is kept by praising God with music and prayer, and also by rest from labor. We have seen the religious ceremonies followed in the home and will soon share those of the synagogue; but first let us glance over the laws which meant that the Sabbath should be a day not only for praise of God but for leisure for man.

Thirty-nine kinds of work are forbidden on the Sabbath. One of the most important is the making of a fire, which in early days was real labor. Following this commandment, the mother in the home we have just visited did no cooking on the Sabbath day; although fires for the sake of warmth may be kindled in winter by a non-Jew. The father, you may have noticed, did not smoke. There is no work connected with smoking; but lighting his cigar or pipe is forbidden.

Of course, just to keep the Sabbath by doing no work would be dull and stupid. The Jews have always encouraged pleasures that will make the Sabbath day a real joy and not a burden. But these pleasures should not keep one from the synagogue, for the Jew has always said: "I rejoiced when they said unto me, Let us go to the house of the Lord." In the old days, the house of the Lord was the great Temple in Jerusalem; today it is the synagogue. So before we accompany our friends to the synagogue for the Sabbath service, let us see how the first synagogues began.

The magnificent temple built by King Solomon at Jerusalem was destroyed by the soldiers of Nebuchadnezzar, and the mourning Jews were carried off into their seventy-year long captivity in Babylon. In this far-off land the exiles learned that it was possible to worship God outside of the great national shrine in Jerusalem, and they gathered together for prayer and comfort. When the Jews returned to their land, Ezra called an assembly of all the people that they might hear the Laws of Moses read to them. He and the other religious leaders stood upon a platform, which was called a BIMA; we still have it in our synagogues today. Later a new Temple rose in Jerusalem; this Second Temple was later beautified and enlarged by King Herod. But although the Jewish people again came to the Temple for worship, they continued to meet in smaller groups for prayers and study. Such a meeting place was called in Hebrew BETH-HA-KENESETH, house of meeting. Later on, the Jews adopted the Greek form, Synagogue.

When the Second Temple was destroyed by the Romans, it was impossible to carry on the sacrifices which had once been offered daily upon its altars; at the same time the class of COHANIM, or priests, who with the Levites had served in the Temple, no longer had any special work to do. But in the synagogues, scattered first through Palestine, later wherever Jews lived, prayer and study came to take the place of sacrifice; while the rabbis, or teachers, became the religious leaders of the Jewish people.

Now we understand how very ancient the Synagogue is. For example, when we enter ours this Sabbath and look up at the MAGEN DAVID above the door we will see a dec-

Magen David

oration which is so old that no one knows just when it began. These two triangles form a star, and for some unknown reason are called the Shield of David; it would be interesting to write down a list of all the places where you have seen this old, old symbol, both in the synagogue and in the Jewish home.

During the World War the Magen David was used instead of a cross as a marker for the American Jewish soldiers buried in France. And you may be interested to learn that instead of being called the Red Cross, a Jewish society formed to help the sick and wounded was called the Red Magen David and used the double triangle as its emblem.

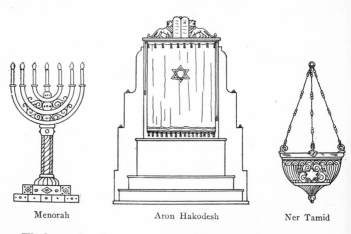

Menorah   Aron Hakodesh   Ner Tamid

We have already learned that the Bima, or speaker's stand, has come down from very early days. In many synagogues there are two platforms, one for the reading of the Torah and one for holding the Ark, which contains the Torah. Today we often find just one platform with its two desks. Another feature of the synagogue is the women's gallery. In Palestine and later in other eastern countries, the Jews followed the Oriental custom of separating the women from the men, and reserved a screened place for them in the gallery. Today, especially in small synagogues, the women often have their place in a special section on the main floor.

The most important thing we will see in the synagogue we visit today is the Ark. The Ark is a sort of closet or chest to contain the Scrolls of the Law. It is placed in the wall toward which the congregation and its leader, either the hazan or rabbi, turn when they pray. You remember the Mizrach in the Jewish home which marked the eastern wall? In the synagogue the Jews also turn toward the east in prayer that they may face Jerusalem. Several steps lead up to the Ark; above it are two tablets, with the abbreviations of the first two words

The Two Tablets

of each of the Ten Commandments upon them. A richly embroidered velvet curtain covers the Ark; the NER TAMID hangs before it. This is a lamp, usually of an ancient pattern; it is the everlasting light and represents the brightness which comes from the Torah to fill the world with the light of God's teachings. It is never allowed to go out. Light also comes from the two large menorahs with their eight branches.

The Sephardic Jews, whose ancestors were driven from Spain in the year Columbus discovered America, allow the curtains of the Ark to remain open. This goes back to those terrible days of persecution, when they were obliged to practise their Judaism secretly, and discovery meant imprisonment or death. Fearing that a spy might be hidden behind the curtains to listen to them repeating their forbidden prayers, these Marranos (secret Jews) drew back the velvet hangings. But the Askenazim (German and Polish Jews) draw aside the curtains only when the Sefer Torah is shown, or taken out to be read to the congregation.

The Torah

Sefer is the Hebrew for book; a Sefer Torah contains the five books of Moses written in Hebrew upon a scroll of parchment. (You remember the tiny Mezuzah, which is also written on parchment and rolled like an ancient scroll before the days of printing.) Of course the Sofer, who copies the Sefer Torah, must be a very pious as well as a very learned man; he must know not only Hebrew, but just what kind of parchment to use; he must see that the sheets of parchment are all the right size and that the sinews of the right animal (clean according to Jewish law) bind them together. The sticks upon which the parchment is rolled are either wood, ivory, or silver. The Sefer Torah is wrapped in linen, silk or velvet; another cover is then placed over it, usually of velvet, and like the curtains of the Ark, decorated with Hebrew letters embroidered in gold. The Magen David is often a part of these decorations. Often the upper ends of the sticks are decorated with gold or silver ornaments, shaped like crowns, and sometimes with bells attached; another royal decoration is the shield or breastplate, hanging by a chain. Across the shield hangs the pointer; it is called the YAD, because it is shaped like a small hand and is used by the reader of the Torah to point out the words as he pronounces them. Often the breastplate is made beautiful with gold figures of lions; two lions are often shown above the Ark as well; they are the symbol of strength and represent the Tribe of Judah.

Yad

Taking the Torah from the Ark is one of the most beautiful ceremonies in the synagogue. I am sure Miriam and David enjoyed it better than any part of the service. They must have felt like the child described in the verses, written by an unknown poet:

The Torah Bells

When dad takes me to Synagogue
  I like to hear the singing,
But most of all I like to hear
  The Torah bells a-ringing.
The pretty little Torah bells
  That tinkle all the way
From up the Ark right to the desk
  Where they are put away.
But only for a little while;
  They read the Sidrah through;
And then the bells go back again
  And the curtains are drawn to.
I like to hear the sermon
  And the tales the preacher tells,
But most of all in Synagogue
  I like the Torah bells.

But let us take the reading of the Torah in the right place in the service. Now we will follow the usual Sabbath service; the services for the various holy days will come later. The first important thing to notice in a synagogue service is its language. Hebrew has always been the language of prayer for the Jewish people, no matter what language they adopted from their neighbors for use in daily life. In the days when every Jewish boy received only a Hebrew education, and a very thorough one, too, almost every member in the entire congregation could read the Torah, even though it was written without vowels, and could conduct the whole services. A hazan (or cantor) was chosen because of his fine voice; he led the congregation in chanting the prayers. In those days the work of the rabbi was not to deliver sermons but to teach and to answer questions about the Jewish law.

But nowadays there are not many Hebrew scholars in the congregation. Sometimes many of the members cannot even follow the prayers read by the hazan. For this reason in many synagogues the prayers are translated into English that those who do not know enough Hebrew can understand what is being recited. The Jew has always called Hebrew the Sacred Tongue, LASHON HAKODESH. Jews from every part of the globe have been joined together by the golden chain of their ancient common language when they prayed. It is a fine thing when a Jewish boy or girl learns Hebrew, not only for his bar mitzvah and confirmation exercises, but that all through his life he can pray and sing in the language of his fathers.

The most important part of the public as well as the private prayers of the Jew is the SHEMA, with which every Jewish child is familiar before he attends synagogue. The next is the AMIDA, sometimes called the SHEMONE ESRE. This prayer not only asks God for help and guidance but also praises and thanks Him for His goodness. Public prayers are offered three times a day, in the morning, afternoon, and at sundown. On the Sabbath, New Moon, and Festivals other prayers are added, some of which we will note as we study the holy days.

Another important part of the service is the taking out of the Torah to read to the congregation. Seven males are called up to the leader's platform for the reading of the Law; as his part for the day is read, each of these men repeats as an introduction the following blessing in Hebrew: "Praise ye the Lord, Who is to be praised; praised be the Lord, Who is to be praised forever and aye. Praised art Thou, O Lord, our God, King of the World, Who has chosen us from among all nations, and has given us His law. Praised art Thou, O Lord, Giver of the law." In the old days, every man honored by being called up to the Torah read a section to the congregation. Later because fewer people were learned in Hebrew and found it difficult to read without vowels, the appointed reader read the whole portion for that day. We have seen an exception to this rule when a boy is bar mitzvah; now we understand what

INTERIOR OF THE GREAT SYNAGOGUE AT BOKHARA

an honor falls to him on that day. Another old custom is observed by following a set order of calling members of the congregation up to the platform; first we have a Cohen, one who comes from the priestly family of Aaron; next a descendant of Levi, the tribe who served in the Temple; then six others who are thought to belong to the other tribes of Israel and are known simply as Israelites. The eighth man is called "Maftir," the one who is to conclude; he also reads the prophetic portion of the day.

The Torah is read not only on the Sabbath day, but also on Mondays and Thursdays, a custom said to go back to the time of Ezra, when Jews outside of Jerusalem, unable to make the journey on the Sabbath, came to the city for the reading of the Law. The Torah is the name given to the five books of Moses; the portions of the prophets, which follow the Torah readings, are called HAFTARAH, which means conclusion.

Certain old and well-known songs are sung as part of the services. "ADON OLOM" is one of them which you may have heard sung in the synagogue at the beginning or end of the service. Here are several stanzas from the translation Israel Zangwill made of this hymn:

ADON OLOM (LORD OF THE WORLD)

Lord of the world, He reigned alone
  While yet the universe was naught,
  When by His will all things were wrought,
Then first His sovran name was known.

He is the living God to save,
  My Rock while sorrow's toils endure,
  My banner and my stronghold sure,
The cup of life whene'er I crave.

I place my soul within His palm
  Before I sleep as when I wake,
  And though my body I forsake,
Rest in the Lord in fearless calm.

Another hymn of the synagogue which states the main beliefs of Judaism as expressed by the greatest of Jewish philosophers, Maimonides, is "YIGDAL." Here are a few lines:

YIGDAL (THE LIVING GOD)

The living God we praise, exalt, adore!
He was, He is, He will be evermore.
Lord of the Universe is He proclaimed,
Teaching His power to all His hand has framed.

We have already mentioned one of the loveliest of Sabbath hymns, "Come, my Beloved," which we heard sung in the Jewish home on Friday night; another well-known synagogue hymn is "EN KELOHENU" (There is none like our God!) which you have all sung in the religious school.

The choir in most synagogues is made up entirely of men and boys. As it was once thought improper for men and women to sing together in public, boys whose voices had not yet matured were chosen for the soprano parts. We have already spoken of the hazan, a skilled musician who chants the prayers. There is no organ in the orthodox synagogue. In the old days many musical instruments were used in the Temple service at Jerusalem; but with the destruction of the Temple, the rabbis decided that as a sign of mourning no instrumental music should be played as part of the synagogue services.

Once David and Miriam attended a Reform Temple. They noticed several changes from the synagogue to which they had always gone with their father. Men and women instead of being separated, sat together in family pews; there was an organ and a choir of both men and women. Instead of having a hazan chant the prayers, they were read by the rabbi. The men, instead of keeping on their hats, worshipped with bare heads.

But the children also noticed how the two places of worship resembled each other: the Magen David, the Ark with its Sefer Torah, the Ner Tamid were all the same. Although less Hebrew was used, the prayers were much the same and the same hymns were sung, hymns, which like the Shema, express the most important idea in Judaism, the greatness and unity of God. David thought it all out during the reading of the Torah; later he spoke to his father about it.

"Although all Jews do not keep the same customs," said David, "it seem to me that the whole Jewish people are all bound together by their belief in one God and their long history. When we say the 'Shema' we are one, just as God is one."

"Our rabbis had a beautiful saying that 'All Israel are brothers'," answered David's father.

SOMETHING TO ASK YOURSELVES

1. Give two reasons for observing the Sabbath. Give two ways in which it should be observed.
2. When and why did the Synagogue begin?
3. Tell what ceremonial objects you see in the Synagogue.
4. Describe the Ark and the Sefer Torah.
5. Name the two most important prayers of every public service. The most important hymns.
6. How do services differ in the orthodox and reform synagogues? How do they resemble each other?

SOMETHING TO DO

1. Do you know that three Sabbaths are kept in Palestine? Write an essay describing how the followers of three world religions keep their Sabbath day; show also how all peoples have found it necessary to observe a rest day.
2. There are stories of the building of the Temple at Jerusalem which you will want to read and retell to the class. Why King Solomon decided to build the first Temple on Mount

Zion is told in "The Field of Brotherly Love" in the collection
of stories, *The Heaven on the Sea*. The legend of King Herod's
share in the Second Temple may be found in *Story of the
Jewish People* (Vol. I) or *Great Jews Since Bible Days*.

3.   Look up and bring to class, pictures of synagogues in
Europe and this country. If you know an architect, ask him
to what style of architecture these various synagogues belong.

4.   Ask your rabbi to take the class about the synagogue to
study the various ceremonial objects described in this chapter.
Perhaps he may be willing to take the Sefer Torah from the
Ark that you may see the unpointed Hebrew writing for yourselves. (If you have studied Hebrew you will realize what a
help the vowels are!)

5.   There are many stories about the Shema; it has been the
death cry of Jewish martyrs through the ages; in war, soldiers
have learned that a fallen enemy was a fellow-Jew by hearing
him repeat the "watchword of Israel." Can you write a short
original story about the Shema? Or a poem to show what it
has always meant to the Jew?

6.   Maimonides wrote the Thirteen Articles of Faith which
express what a Jew believes. Read a rhymed translation of
Yigdal and compare. Dr. Kohler's *Guide for Instruction in
Judaism* contains the Thirteen Articles. There are poetic
translations of Yigdal in *The Standard Book of Jewish Verse*
(Friedlander) and *Services in Synagogue and Home* (Dembitz); unfortunately both of these fine books are out of print;
but you may find a copy in your school library.

SOMETHING TO READ

1.   There is a story called "Sabbath" by Eliezar David
Rosenthal in *Yiddish Tales*, translated by Helena Frank. It is
very sad, but you may want to read it as a study in Jewish life.

2.   You will find verses on the synagogue and Jewish prayer in any of the collections I have named before, especially
on the Torah—but you may want to keep them for our study
of Simchath Torah.

VIII

THE AUTUMN FESTIVALS

"Tomorrow is Rosh Hashanah," Miriam told her school friend Mary, "so I'm going to stay home from school."

"I remember you did last year. But wasn't it the end of September, and tomorrow is only the twelfth? Do Jewish people have a different date for their holidays every year?"

"It looks as though we did," answered Miriam doubtfully. "But I don't know why. I'll have to ask my father." She did ask him that night over the apples and honey on the Rosh Hashanah dinner table. You may want to listen too; for even if you cannot share the good things to eat, you may care to hear a little about the Jewish calendar.

The JEWISH CALENDAR is based upon the moon; each month is either twenty-nine or thirty days. The new moon always shows that a new month has begun. But twelve months according to the moon do not make up the total of 365 days, which is the time it takes for the earth to go around the sun; a lunar year (one by the moon) would be too short, and in a few years all the seasons would be turned around. So every two or three years the Jewish calendar has a leap year and a whole month is added; in this way it catches up and is never more than a few days ahead or behind the civil calendar.

Jews do not number the years from a great event in their own religion, like the Christians and the Mohammedans, but from the very beginning of the world, as near as the ancient rabbis could figure it out. So the year 1928-1929 of the civil calendar, in which I am writing this book, is 5689 in the Jewish calendar.

The first of every Jewish month is celebrated as a half holiday, the Rosh Hodesh or New Moon. At one time it was customary to pronounce the blessing for the New Moon in the open air, facing the crescent, in a group of not less than ten. Nowadays this blessing is usually read in the synagogue. Women are given a holiday from household tasks on this day because of the legend that in the time of Moses and Aaron they were less willing than the men to worship the Golden Calf.

Nisan is really the first month of the Jewish year, because it marked the exodus from Egypt, the beginning of a free, national life for Israel. But in celebrating the Jewish festivals with Miriam and her brother David, we will begin with the fall holy days and the celebration of the Jewish New Year, the first festival recorded in the Luach (tablet), or Jewish calendar.

Rosh Hashanah, which means "head (or beginning) of the year," falls in the seventh month, Tishri. It is also called the Day of the Blowing of the Shofar, the Day of Memorial, and the Day of Judgment. Like all the other Jewish festivals it begins on the eve of the holy day. You may be sure that David and Miriam were ready early in the afternoon, dressed in their best, ready to take their places at the dinner table, set with Challah and lighted candles. After father had pronounced a special holiday blessing, they did not need a second invitation before they began to dip their apples into the honey and eat it up just as fast as they could to be sure of a sweet year.

"But it will be a sweet and happy year only if we make it so," said father. "Next January first you will be wishing your Christian friends a happy New Year. But we Jews say—"

"*Leshanah tovah tikasevu,*" interrupted David, and I am

sorry to say his mouth was so full that nobody understood him.

"I know what that means," piped up little Joe, their six-year-old orphan cousin who had come to live with them. "It means, 'May you be written down for a good year.' It's always printed on New Year cards."

"You see, Rosh Hashanah begins a new year for us," explained father. "Jews hope to have their names written down in the Book of Life. And a good year means more than a sweet year or a happy one; we want the next twelve months to be filled with good deeds; for our year will be good only if we help to make it so ourselves."

"I guess that's why it is called the Day of Remembrance, or Memorial," said David, "a day to remember all the things we have done the last year, that we can see where we have made mistakes and plan to do better next time."

"Yes, it is a day for judging ourselves," agreed father. "You see there are a number of names for Rosh Hashanah. It is the Day of Memorial (Yom Hazikaron), not only to remember our own acts but for the remembrance of all things that have happened since the beginning of time. It is the Day of Judgment (Yom Hadin) on which we judge our own acts and pray to God to judge us in mercy and forgiveness. And can anybody tell me another name for Rosh Hashanah?"

"The Day of the Blowing of the Shofar," cried Miriam.

"In old days," went on father, "the shofar, or ram's horn, was blown to call the soldiers from their tents to do battle for Israel. It was also used on solemn occasions to bring the people together for judgment. The shofar was

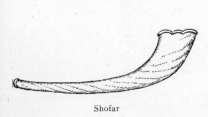

Shofar

also blown when the children of Israel received the Ten Commandments at Sinai; it was sounded as part of the ceremony of the New Moon every month. It is very likely that in olden times it was made of the curved horn of the wild goat in remembrance of the story of Abraham."

"When Abraham was going to sacrifice Isaac and found a ram in the thicket to take his place on the altar?" asked little Joe.

"Yes. The story of Abraham's obedience to God is always read in the synagogue on the second day of Rosh Hashanah as an example to Israel who must always be obedient and willing to sacrifice everything at God's command. Year after year we hear this story and remember how many Jews in our long, hard history have followed Abraham's example. Year after year on the first day of Rosh Hashanah we sing the dying prayer of Rabbi Amnon, who in the end was brave enough to die for his religion. But, of course, the most important ceremony we have on New Year's is the blowing of the shofar."

"Don't forget TASHLICH," spoke up the children's mother. "On Rosh Hashanah afternoon, we walk to the river and empty our pockets into the water or throw crumbs into the stream. This is called Tashlich, from the Hebrew word cast, because the prophet Micah speaks of God casting the sins of Israel into the sea. Of course, no one believes we are throwing away our wickedness with the crumbs; but it helps us to remember through the year that we really want to put away our sins and lead better lives."

"But why do we keep two days Rosh Hashanah"? asked Joe.

"That is rather a long story," answered father. "You know that the Jewish calendar is based on the moon; each new month began when the crescent moon was seen and reported by trustworthy witnesses. Then messengers could be sent, or signal fires lighted upon the hills, so that everyone in the little land

of Palestine could know that the new month had begun. But
when Jews began to scatter through Egypt and Greece and
other lands it was impossible without telegrams to let everybody know the exact time. So to be absolutely sure, the Jews
outside of Palestine kept two days for all of the important
festivals except Yom Kippur. Later a calendar was established
and the exact date of every holy day was fixed; but the Jews
outside of Palestine still followed the tradition of keeping the
second day as a reminder that they were no longer living in the
land of their fathers."

"Why isn't Yom Kippur kept for two days?" demanded
Miriam.

"Because the rabbis realized that fasting would be too severe
for many people if they had to keep two days," answered
father. "A day is quite long enough, as David who is just
old enough, will find out by Yom Kippur."

YOM KIPPUR, as most of you know, falls on the tenth of
Tishri. During the Ten Days of Penitence which begin with
Rosh Hashanah and end with the evening of Yom Kippur, the
faithful Jew has plenty of time to prepare himself for the most
solemn of all Jewish holy days. During this time many Jews
offer special prayers at their early morning services, asking forgiveness for any sins they may have committed during the
year. It is the time not only for making one's peace with God
but with man. A Jew who during this period recalls a wrong
he has done any one should ask pardon for his fault; if he himself has been wronged he must forgive his brother just as he
expects God to forgive him on this solemn day of confession
and pardon.

The rabbis said that during these Ten Days God kept the
Book of Life spread out before Him that He might enter on its
pages the names of those who through repentance and right-
living deserved forgiveness. The Sabbath that falls during the

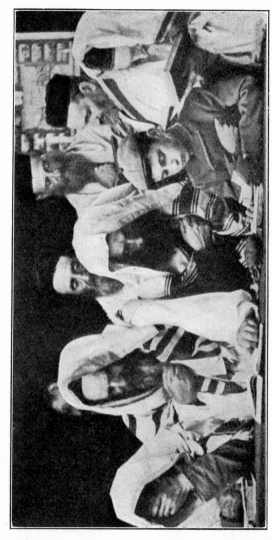

DAY OF ATONEMENT IN AN ORTHODOX SYNAGOGUE

Ten Days is called SHABBAS SHUVAH (the Sabbath of Return) and on that day a chapter from the prophet Isaiah is read in the synagogue, beginning with the word Shuvah, and urging Israel to return to God.

Even little Joe knew that Yom Kippur was a very solemn day. His uncle had told him how long ago special sacrifices were offered up in the Temple at Jerusalem by the high priest, dressed in white linen garments, with a glittering breast plate and towering cap. One of these sacrifices was of two goats; the one selected by lot was set apart for the Lord; the other, the scapegoat, was pronounced the sin-offering of the entire nation and driven outside of the city to the waste places beyond Jerusalem by the high priest, just as the people desired to drive sin from their midst. Jews have no animal sacrifices today, although there is a survival of this very ancient custom in the ceremony of KAPOROTH (atonement) by which a fowl is killed, a rooster for a man, a hen for a woman.

Another Yom Kippur custom which especially interested Miriam was the Dance in the Vineyards. Her father pictured for her Yom Kippur afternoon in ancient Jerusalem, the brightly clothed maidens swaying in the dance, the youths looking on. That no poor girl need feel ashamed of her plain garments, on this day rich girls exchanged their festal robes with their poorer sisters. When the dance was over, many a young man would step forward to claim the maiden of his choice who later became his bride.

But in our time there is no merrymaking on Yom Kippur. The feeling of solemnity which this holy day brings is sounded on the eve of Yom Kippur in the beautiful melody, KOL NIDRE. On this day the Jew ends his season of self-examination by confessing his sins before God and asking for His forgiveness. He does not fast as a punishment; but he wishes to prove to himself that as the body can abstain from food, the soul can keep itself free from temptations during the coming year. Although a solemn day, Yom Kippur is not a sad one, in spite of the Memorial Service in which the names of those who have died are recalled. In some congregations the men and boys past bar mitzvah, and considered old enough to fast all day instead of a few hours, wear shrouds; but this is not in sign of mourning. They are not only to remind the worshippers that Death waits for every man and should be met proudly with the remembrance of a life well-lived; these white garments signify the purity of the soul and God's forgiveness. In some congregations only the rabbi wears a large shroud-like talith in remembrance of this custom.

This day of prayer and fasting and meditation and confession comes to an end with the impressive NEILAH (concluding) service. In the Temple at Jerusalem when the High Priest entered the Holy of Holies, that place which even he might enter only during this part of the Yom Kippur service, the entire congregation prostrated themselves upon the ground as before a king. Today the rabbi or hazan bows low before the Ark reciting the last words of the service. The Gates of Heaven close slowly; it is sunset; and Yom Kippur is over.

Now what do you think a Jew is supposed to do as soon as he goes home from the synagogue on Yom Kippur and eats his supper? He goes out into his yard and drives a stake into the ground for his Succah! Of course he could wait a few days, as it does not take long to build a Succah, anyhow. But this is certainly a beautiful way of showing that he enjoys the Jewish holy days so much that as soon as he is through with one he begins to plan for another.

Miriam and David and Joe always liked SUCCOTH best of all the fall holy days. They could never decide which was the most fun, helping father build the Succah, going to the country for boughs for the roof, or eating in it afterwards. The SUCCAH, as everybody knows, is a booth, built by Jews even today in memory of the rude dwellings the Children of Israel built for themselves in the Wilderness. Later when the wanderers were established in the Promised Land they built these little huts to live in while they gathered the fall harvest. This was the time of the great autumn pilgrimage to Jerusalem; the festival was called Succoth, or the Feast of Booths.

"Every male Israelite was expected to make this pilgrimage to Jerusalem three times a year," father explained, as he hammered busily on the family Succah. "There were two other pilgrim feasts we still keep today, the first in early spring for Passover, the next for the barley harvest at Shabuoth. Succoth was the third, with the fall offering of grapes and late wheat. Whenever possible, the mothers, the older children and the servants accompanied the fathers, traveling from every corner of Palestine to the Temple in Jerusalem, carrying their offerings and singing their pilgrim songs. After the offerings were laid upon the altar, there were special prayers for the rain and dew so necessary for the crops during the coming year. The people gathered at the brook Kishon and held the Feast of the Water Pouring there; water was poured upon the ground to represent the downpour during the rainy season, which begins in Palestine directly after Succoth. There were also processions with torches; or the pilgrims carried palms and branches of the willow tree."

"But how could Jews keep on having Succoth festivals when they lost the Temple and they didn't have any crops to bring to it, anyhow?" asked little Joe.

"That is one of the most remarkable things in Jewish history!" answered his uncle. "Do you remember, children, that picture Miss Sampter gives of the Jews locked in their ghetto keeping their Succoth festival, remembering Palestine and dreaming of planting their own fields and vineyards again?"

"Yes, I learned it for the Succoth program last year," answered Miriam. And she recited:

THE LULAB

We live in narrow alleys
   Where hovels stand in rows—
Our hearts are in the valleys
   Where Rose of Sharon grows.

From bartering, peddling, selling
   We seek a moment's calm—
Our hearts today are dwelling
   Where citron grows with palm.

We come from stinting, suffering,
   From streets that pennies yield;
And bring the Lord our offering,
   The produce of the field.

Unlanded, robbed, and driven,
   And happy to escape,
Our dreams today are given
   To farm and flock and grape.

In many a stone-bound city,
   Still roofed beneath the skies,
The Lord of boundless pity
   Lets little bowers arise.

And in those tabernacles—
   The wanderer's blessed relief—
He turns our heavy shackles
   To strings of fruit and leaf.

We who bring in want and sorrow
The stranger's fruit with psalms,
Shall plant in joy tomorrow
Their citrons and their palms.

"This was written quite a few years ago," said father, "when there were not so many farm colonies in Palestine. Today there is a wonderful, new life growing up there; young men and women from all over the world are planting and reaping in the old-new land of our fathers; there is even a colony where orphan children are learning to milk their cows and care for their poultry like real farmers."

"And there's the Farm School at Doylestown, Pa.," declared David. "I told my chum about it when he said that Jews were business men and didn't care for farming."

"For a long time that was true," admitted his father, "for Jews were not allowed to hold land and cultivate it. But now if he wishes it, a Jew may be a farmer just as the Jews were when they kept Succoth in old Palestine."

"But you haven't finished our Succah," complained little Joe. "There are some big holes in the top."

His uncle laughed. "We must always leave holes between the branches which cover our Succah," he explained, "to see the stars through. For if we look up at the stars the way our ancestors did in the desert and remember that God guides not only the stars but all of his children on earth, we will not be afraid even if we have to live in a little tent in the wilderness."

Miriam hung her last bunch of grapes and stood off to get the effect. "Isn't it wonderful how all those old ideas have come down to us?" she said, as she began to roll up her ball of twine. "Just like the lulab and the esrog we are going to see in the synagogue tomorrow."

THE SUCCAH
(*Moritz Oppenheimer*)

The LULAB, or palm branch is one of the leading symbols of Succoth. It is bound with the myrtle and the willow. The fourth plant used it also from Palestine, the ESROG, which is a kind of citron. The rabbis have given each plant a different meaning; the one I like the best explains that these four plants are bound together that one may supply the lack in the other. The citron has odor and taste, the palm, which represents the date fruit, only taste; the myrtle has no taste, but is loved for its pleasant odor; while the willow, although it has no virtue of its own, becomes pleasing because it is bound with its brothers, and is aided by them, as a less fortunate Jew is aided when gathered with the rest of Israel.

Lulab and Esrog

This bundle of plants is still waved in the home or the synagogue, usually the later, every day but Saturday of the festival of Succoth, with the benediction: "Blessed art Thou, O Lord our God, King of the World, Who hast sanctified us by Thy commandments, and hast given us command concerning the taking of the lulab." Whenever possible these plants are sent from Palestine; although during the Golden Age of Jewry in Spain, Jews in other parts of Europe kept Succoth with the palms and citrons from that country. Later, Spanish Jews, who had been exiled to Salonica, remembered their old homeland by using a lulab sent from Spain.

The seventh day of Succoth is known as the day of the Great Hoshannah (prayers beginning with Hoshannah "save us"). Hoshannahs are recited in the synagogue, and a custom going back to Bible times is repeated. The pilgrims to Jerusalem formed a great procession on that day and walked about the altar shaking the branches they carried. It is thought that the trembling leaves suggested rain needed for the next crops; today willow branches called "Hoshannahs" are shaken during the reading of these prayers.

Although the uncertain autumn climate in America made it impossible for our family to eat all their meals in their Succah for an entire week, they were usually able to gather there for the evening meal. The children were sorry to see their festival draw to an end, when SHEMINI AZERETH, the eighth day of Succoth, came. Shemini Azereth is kept for two days; the second is called SIMCHATH TORAH, one of the most meaningful of all Jewish holy days.

I wonder whether you would care to read part of a little poem I once wrote to tell that Simchath Torah is not only a part of the Harvest Festival, but is a sort of special thanksgiving for the Jew.

SIMCHATH TORAH

It was good to give thanks to the Lord
   For the sun and the rain,
For the corn and the wine He bestowed,
   For the golden-wreathed grain;
But now as the festal week ends,
   'Neath the palms that we wave,
We cry thanks to the Giver of Good,
   For the Torah He gave.

O harvesters, rich in your spoils,
   Not alone by the bread
Which we win by the sweat of our brows
   Are the sons of dust fed;
Nay, we live by the words of His mouth,
   And 'neath palms that we wave,
We cry thanks to the Giver of Good
   For the Torah He gave.

REJOICING IN THE TORAH
(*Moritz Oppenheimer*)

Simchath Torah means rejoicing in the Torah; once a year in a special festival the Jew thanks God for this gift even more precious than the harvest. On this day the Jewish people rejoice that they have finished reading the entire Torah in the weekly Sabbath service. But the reader immediately turns back to the beginning and reads the first chapter of Genesis. An ancient legend tells us that if the Evil One saw the Jews rejoicing on this day he would think they were happy that they had completed their duty. But Satan is confused when he finds that the real cause of their happiness is their delight in beginning to read their Book anew. He knows that there is no use in hoping that the Jew will ever weary in his study of his Book of Books.

In an earlier chapter you have read how the first day of the Jewish school child was sweetened with honey cakes that he might learn the delight of the Torah. This custom was repeated on Simchath Torah when nuts and sweetmeats were scattered for the children to scramble for and enjoy. Another pleasure, which has come down to our own day, is the procession marching seven times around the synagogue, in which the school boys are allowed to join. This procession is led by the rabbi and leading men of the congregation each of them carrying a Sefer Torah. The boys follow, carrying flags which they have made themselves; often they have lighted candles at the ends of their staves. As the scrolls are carried down the aisles, the rest of the congregation lean forward to kiss them in reverence.

For the Torah has always been the peculiar treasure of the Jewish people. It has been their Ner Tamid, the light which will never die. Cruel tyrants often burned the Torah; but the Jews, who stood by helpless and weeping, carried its message in their hearts until happier times when they might again study in peace. During the World War groups of refugee Jews, driven forth into exile, carried their Torahs in their arms, often the one treasure they had saved from their wrecked homes. In some of the large Jewish centers like Warsaw, special places were set aside for the safekeeping of these scrolls until a day of peace should dawn for Israel and the world. And today many of these scrolls are again read with gratitude and rejoicing in the restored Jewish communities all over Europe, in the colonies of the Ukraine and of Palestine.

Simchath Torah is one of the minor holy days. But no other Jewish festival expresses so well the Jew's devotion to his Torah, which has given him comfort and wisdom and life itself, through the long and terrible years of his exile.

SOMETHING TO ASK YOURSELF

1. Describe the Jewish calendar. Describe the festival of the New Moon.

2. What is the meaning of Rosh Hashanah? Give the other three names of this holy day and explain the meaning of each one.

3. What Bible story is always read in the synagogue for Rosh Hashanah? Why?

4. Describe the ceremony of Tashlich.

5. Why are the major holy days kept two days? Which one is excepted? Why?

6. What are the Ten Days of Penitence? What is the meaning of Shabbas Shuvah?

7. Describe two ceremonies of Yom Kippur in the days when the Temple stood.

8. What is a Succah and when and why is it built?

9. Name the three great Pilgrim feasts.

10. What plants are used in the Succoth service? Do you know their meaning?

11. For what is the Jew grateful on Simchath Torah? How is this holy day celebrated?

Something to Do

1. Make a Luach with the Jewish names of the months and each holy day marked in its place. This would be a fine present for a parent or teacher.

2. Decorate a Rosh Hashanah card. If you cannot draw well, cut out a Jewish picture and paste it on for decoration. A picture of Abraham and Isaac would be appropriate. Why? Write the usual New Year greeting in Hebrew characters.

3. Write a Succoth story or one-act play. You might tell the story of some modern children building a Succah; or go back to Bible times and show the Succoth pilgrimage to Jerusalem.

4. Make a flag for Simchath Torah with some distinctive Jewish design like the Magen David, or a Sefer Torah.

5. Learn a poem about one of the holy days studied in this chapter. There are two given here; you will find many others in any of the collections of poetry mentioned before. One of the loveliest is "Yom Kippur" by Gustav Gottheil; a Succoth poem you will like is "Palm and Myrtle" by Eleazar Kali.

Something to Read

1. Even in such a long chapter you cannot find out everything about the holy days. If you like to read rather hard, grown-up books, turn to the reference books for teachers at the end of this volume. Israel Abrahams in his *Festival Studies* has essays on "The Shofar" and "By the Water Side" for Rosh Hashanah. All of these books will help you understand the beauty not only of the Tishri holy days, but also of those that follow.

2. Get out your Bibles and read: the story of the sacrifice of Isaac (Genesis 22) and how the Tishri holy days were kept in Bible times. (For Rosh Hashanah: Numbers 10:10; Numbers 29:11; Yom Kippur, Leviticus 16; Leviticus 23:26-32; Succoth, Leviticus 23:38-43). There are fascinating legends of the sacrifice of Isaac in Ginzberg's *Legends of the Jews*, Vol. I.

3. "If Not Higher" is a story which you will enjoy reading around Rosh Hashanah. It was written by Perez; translations

may be found in *A Book of Jewish Thoughts* (Hertz) and *Stories and Pictures* (Frank).

4. A good Yom Kippur story, "A Tale of Rabbi Israel Salanter" may be found in a collection of Jewish stories, *Worlds that Passed,* by A. S. Sachs. This book also contains descriptions of the other holy days.

5. Other well-known Yom Kippur stories are "Three Who Ate" by David Frischman and "Yom Kippur" by Eliezer David Rosenthal, found in *Yiddish Tales* (Helena Frank).

6. Unfortunately, some of the best holy day stories are written either in Hebrew or Yiddish. If you are not able to read them in the original you may care to read some of mine. There are a great many, as I have specialized in such stories. written especially for children. For Rosh Hashanah and Yom Kippur: "The Man Who Came Late," "The Day of Return" (*In Many Lands*); "A New Year for Berthold," "The Rabbi and the Bishop" (a story of Rabbi Amnon); "The Day of Forgiveness" (*Tales Old and New*); "The Dawn of Freedom," "The Borrowed Garment" (*Playmates in Egypt*); "A New Page," "A Big Mistake" (*Jewish Holyday Stories*).

7. A book you will be sure to enjoy from cover to cover is: *Festival Studies of Childhood in a Jewish Colony in Palestine* by Hannah Trager. Suppose you read first: "New Year's Eve"; "The Day of Atonement."

8. I have already mentioned Miss Ish Kishor's book of stories, *The Heaven on the Sea.* Among the holy day stories you will want to read in it is: "How Bennie Went to Look for the New Year."

9. There is a good account of the Drawing of the Water in Myers' *Story of the Jewish People,* Chapter VIII.

10. Now we are ready for stories for Succoth and Simchath Torah. Here are a few from different books: "Late," Abraham Raisin (*Yiddish Tales*); "The Succoth Bough," Ish Kishor (*Heaven on the Sea*); "Feast of Tabernacles"; "Simchath Torah", Hannah Trager (*Festival Studies*); "Before Dawn," Abraham Isaacs (*Under the Sabbath Lamp*); "The Tabernacle," Sholom Aleichem (*Jewish Children*).

11. My stories for these two holy days are: "His Own Succah" and "The Coward" (*Jewish Holy Day Stories*); "In the Tents of Israel" (*Playmates in Egypt*); "The Tent of Refuge"; "The Flag of My People" (*In Many Lands*); "Max and Herschel—and a Succah"; "The Torah in No Man's Land" (*Tales Old and New.*)

IX

THE WINTER FESTIVALS

Outside the wintry wind blew gusts of snow against the frosted panes; but inside the house all was warm and cheerful. On the window sill stood a brightly burnished Chanukah menorah with candles in two of its nine branches ready to be lighted. Miriam was helping mother put the last touches to the dinner table; David and his little cousin Joseph were hovering over the living room davenport piled with various bundles, pinching the ones marked with their names, in the hope of discovering what was inside.

"I'm afraid there's nothing big enough for a toy aeroplane," mourned David. "And I told father last week that if I got one I wouldn't expect a single other Chanukah present."

"There's father now!" cried Miriam from the doorway. She rushed to meet him and the others followed. "Hurry up! We want to light the candles."

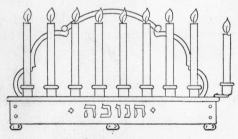

Chanukah Menorah

"Who's going to light the first candle for the first night of Chanukah?" asked father, taking off his snowy overcoat.

87

"I suppose we've got to let Joseph, 'cause he's the youngest," complained David, still unhappy over the toy aeroplane. "He's always the youngest."

"But there are eight nights for lighting the candles," Miriam consoled him, "so we'll all get a chance."

"Why is that candle called the SHAMMAS?" asked Joseph, pointing to the candle which stood a little aside from the rest.

"Shammas means servant," explained his uncle. "You know we call old Mr. Fineberg the shammas of our synagogue because he takes care of it, and always sees that everything is just right for services. The shammas, in a way, is the most important of all the lights, because the other candles receive their light from it. Now, Joseph, let us hear how well you know the blessings."

Mother came in from the kitchen to hear him. Joseph, standing very proud and tall, recited this blessing over the first candle: "Blessed art Thou, O Lord our God, King of the world, Who hast sanctified us by Thy commandments and commanded us to kindle the lights of Chanukah. Blessed art Thou, O Lord our God, King of the world, Who hast wrought miracles for our fathers in days of old at this season."

"The first part's almost like the Shabbas blessing mother says over the candles," Miriam whispered to her brother.

"Ssh!" David told her. "He's got more to say 'cause it's the first night," and he spoke rather crossly.

So Joseph added the extra blessing for the first night of Chanukah: "Blessed art Thou, O Lord our God, King of the world, Who hast given us life, hast sustained us, and permitted us to see this day." Then, with the brightly shining shammas he lit the first of the Chanukah candles.

"Now let's sing MOOZ T'ZUR," cried Dave, glad to have some part in the service. So they all joined in the old Hebrew song, which I am sure my readers know so well that I do not have to set it down here.

"Isn't it about time for presents?" hinted Miriam.

Everybody was satisfied when the strings were untied, even David; for didn't he get the finest stamp album he had ever seen, and didn't he have right in his pocket a stamp on a letter his Hebrew teacher had written him from Palestine? He was so busy looking for just the right place for it that mother had to call him twice to the dinner table. "Of course, if you don't want any Chanukah pancakes and cheese . . ." she said, but David didn't need any more urging. It was a very special Yomtov supper, and things always tasted just a little better with the menorah shining away in the window.

"Why do we light the candles on Chanukah?" asked little Joe, passing his plate for his third pancake. "I remember Judas Maccabeus and the fighting from last year; but I forget what my Hebrew teacher said about Chanukah being a middle of the winter holiday, or something."

"He must have told you that a great many of the Jewish holy days have what is called an historical and a nature origin," explained his uncle. "Let's take the nature side of the festival first. In the middle of the winter when it is cold and dark, what do we miss the most?"

"The sun," chorused the children.

"Right! A great many nations have celebrated the winter solstice, when we have the longest night and shortest day of the year. The days begin to be longer, just a little more each day. So even the middle of December is a promise of the warm, pleasant days of spring. The Druids in England, for example, used to light great bonfires about this time to represent the sun as they welcomed the longer days."

"But what about the history side?" demanded David.

THE CHANUKAH FESTIVAL
(*Moritz Oppenheimer*)

"There was Judas Maccabeus and the fighting against the Syrians."

"I am just coming to that," smiled father. "When Alexander the Great, who had conquered Palestine, died, he left this province to one of his generals. A Syrian ruled over the Jews. There would have been no trouble, if the mad king Antiochus had not interfered with the religion of his Jewish subjects. Even the Jews who were willing to join in the Greek games and wear Greek clothes and speak the Greek language, even these Jews were angry when Antiochus commanded them to put up statues of the Greek gods in the Temple of Jerusalem. Antiochus not only ordered the Jews to worship his gods but forbade them to keep the two great covenants which had for so long set them apart as Jews—the observance of Sabbath and the rite of circumcision. But the Jews could not be frightened into deserting their own religion. Some of them actually allowed the enemy to cut them down rather than fight upon the Sabbath; parents circumcised their babies, although when such disobedience was discovered they were put to death. The Temple at Jerusalem was desecrated by the Syrian king and his soldiers; they erected statues of their hateful gods in the holy place; they sacrificed swine's flesh upon the altar and tried to force the Jews to eat this forbidden food."

"But the old scribe Eleazar wouldn't," interrupted David, "and he was put to death."

"Like the story of Hannah and her sons," added Miriam. "Just think, Joey, she had seven sons, and the youngest wasn't any older than you. But when Antiochus told them he would give them fine presents if they worshipped his gods, they all refused, even the youngest, and he had them all killed."

"They were the first martyrs for religious liberty," said father. "Up to that time a conquered people had always been willing to accept the gods of their conquerors and worship

them along with their own. Their religion was called poly-
theism, the belief in many gods. But the Jews were monothe-
ists; they believed in one God and would worship no other.
Think of that, children, when you repeat the Shema. You belong to a people who for thousands of years have not only
believed in the oneness of God, but were always ready to die
to proclaim His unity."

"They were ready to fight, too," cried David. "I like
Hannah and her sons; but it's more exciting to read about
Judas Maccabeus and his soldiers."

"I'm afraid war and soldiers are always more interesting to
boys," answered his father a little sadly, and the others knew
he was thinking of his young soldier-brother who had fallen in
France during the World War. "But I want you to remember
that these soldiers were not fighting for more power or more
land. They were the first people in the world to fight for a
man's right to worship his own God as he believed right. I
don't need to tell you the story of the Maccabees; even little
Joe here knows it from the plays he has seen at Hebrew
School. You all remember how Mattathias, an old priest of
Modin, started the rebellion against Antiochus with his battle
cry, 'Those who are on the Lord's side follow me.' The Jewish people rallied to the flag that Judas, his warrior son, rais-
ed; it bore the letters   מכבי   which are the initials of 'Who
is like unto Thee among all the gods?' Having such a cause
to fight for, these half-starved soldiers, with no military training and few weapons, dared to face the veteran armies of Antiochus. For three long years they fought a desperate and
cruel war, as unevenly matched as our own American Revo-
lutionary War against England. But Judas Maccabeus, the
George Washington of the Jewish people, conquered at last.
The Syrians were driven from the land and the Temple was
taken from the enemy. It was cleansed, the statues of the

Greek gods were broken, and the holy place rededicated to God. That is what the word Chanukah means—the Feast of the Rededication."

"It's called the Feast of Lights, too," piped up Joe, glad to show he knew something about the holiday.

"Yes. Chanukah is the Feast of Lights, not only to welcome back the sun, but to celebrate the victory of the Jewish people against the powers of darkness that almost overcame them. When the Temple was ready for rededication, the priests found only one little cruse of oil that was still sealed and unpolluted by the enemy. They used this to light the great menorah, fearing it would burn for just a little while, and sent swift messengers to get more oil. But the lights in the Temple burned until the messengers returned with fresh oil—eight days long."

"That's why we keep Chanukah for eight days," put in Miriam.

"And burn candles to remember the menorah in the Temple," added David. "But why do we begin with one light and go on adding one more every night until every one is burning? Why don't we light them all at once?"

Father smiled. "That is a very old story. Long ago in Jerusalem there lived two great teachers, Hillel and Shammai. They were both so wise and respected that they became leaders of the Jewish people, who belonged either to the school of Hillel or the school of Shammai. Shammai said we should begin the Chanukah celebration by lighting all the candles in the menorah, lighting one taper less each evening during the feast. But Hillel said we should begin with just one light and add another each night as a sign that man should increase in holiness and good deeds. Well, you see we must belong to the school of Hillel, for every year on the twenty-fifth of *Kislev* we still light the menorah in his way."

"And now I want to give you a very special Chanukah present." Father took from his pocket a small top with Hebrew letters on four of its faces. "I'll give it to the child who can tell me what it is."

"A TRENDEL!" cried the three in one voice.

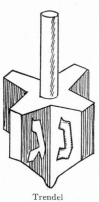

"I lose," said father cheerfully, "and you all win." He reached into his pocket and took out two more. "Here is a trendel for each of you. But before you begin to play with it, who can tell me what the letters mean?"

"I remember from last year," said David, spinning his toy. "They're the initials of four Hebrew words which mean, 'A great miracle happened here.' And you play the game by seeing which letter turns up when you spin."

Trendel

"Father," asked Miriam, as they began to clear the table. "Why do we always have cheese on Chanukah?"

"Because the story of Judith, who saved her people from the enemy just as Judas Maccabeus did, is connected with Chanukah; and the Book of Judith tells us that she brought milk to King Holofernes."

"Did she bring him pancakes, too?" Joey wanted to know. "We always have pancakes and jam for Chanukah." But mother refused to answer. (Sometimes she wished Joe wouldn't ask so many questions!)

As Chanukah is one of the minor festivals, the synagogue services require the addition of certain psalms and prayers in memory of the Maccabean triumph. Mooz T'zur is always sung. But it is one of the great days of the religious school, usually celebrated with a play telling the story of Judas

Maccabeus or Hannah, and featuring the lighting of the menorah.

CHAMISHA ASAR BISHBAT (15th day of SHEBAT), the second of the winter festivals, is also a minor holiday. It is called the New Year of the trees, for when the Jews were farmers in Palestine, they planted new trees on the fifteenth of Shebat and blessed the standing orchards. Fruits which ripened after this date might be offered at the Temple. This festival has been prettily described by the Yiddish writer, Yehoash:

NEW YEAR FOR THE TREES

'Tis a joy-day in the forest;
Since the break of dawn, the soft wind
Blows from tree to tree the tidings:
"Now at last our day is coming!"
All the wood is decked in snow-garb,
Dressed in Rosh Hashanah vesture . . .
And the birdlings, God's musicians,
Gather; melodies are ringing,
"Now at last our day is coming!"
'Tis the joy-day of the wood folks,
Rosh Hashanah in the forest;
Earth and heaven, every creature,
All are crying forth "Good Yomtov."

The trees have always meant a great deal to the Jewish people, not only for fruit, but for shade and beauty. When you remember what a dry land Palestine is, you can understand what the psalmist meant, when he described the reward of the good man by calling him "a tree planted by streams of water." In the days when the Temple stood, there was a beautiful custom of planting a tree before the house at the birth of a child, a cedar for a boy, a cypress for a girl. Sometimes boughs from these trees were used for the framework of their marriage canopy, when they grew up.

After the Romans drove the Jews out of Palestine, the neglected land grew waste and barren. When the first colonists journeyed back to the homeland about fifty years ago they wondered if crops would ever grow there again. It was found that trees would help to save the land. Eucalyptus trees were planted in the swamps and helped to drain them; as the swamps had caused a great deal of malaria, these trees saved many lives; the wood was used for the making of orange boxes, as orange trees proved to be one of the best trees to plant. Now fruit-growing is again one of the leading occupations of Palestine. No wonder the Hebrew poet makes the little colonist children in Palestine sing a

PALESTINE SPRING SONG

Through the wide and verdant meadows
    Lads are bearing plough and hoe;
"Aleph-beth," the master teaches,
    While they saunter to and fro.

Tree, an "aleph"—tree, a "beth"—
    And the "gimel" is a tree;
Trees the symbols, writ on green,
    Far as any eye can see!

Here's the Torah, dearest children;
    Learn its words and hold it dear;
Plant and sow, you merry striplings—
    Look about you—Spring is here!

Study in the book of nature,
    And in all that's written there;
In this land, who plants a sapling
    Flings the flag his comrades bear.

But Jewish children in northern Europe and the United States cannot keep the Jewish arbor day as the children in Palestine keep it, with tree planting and outdoor singing games and dances. As Jessie Sampter describes our wintry climate at Chamisha Asar,

> " . . . Like little feathers covering all,
>   The cold and quiet snowflakes fall."

But she goes on:

> "In my heart there sings a bird
>   And flowers are fair,
> Because I know where blossoms blow,
>   And, oh, my heart is there!
> And there the happy branches bring
> A hope more wonderful than spring."

For Chamisha Asar is one of the most beautiful links that bind us to Palestine. Jewish children who have never seen the land of Israel may celebrate this holiday by eating the fruits that grow there, oranges, figs, dates, and that hard, chewy dainty called bokser, which is the dried fruit of the carob tree. There is a story about the carob tree and the wise but impatient Rabbi Choni, which is always told at Chamisha Asar. But we are in a hurry to get to the next holiday now and if you want to know it you can find the story listed in the references at the end of this chapter. Often children in the religious schools in this country are treated to illustrated lectures about Palestine. Many of them keep the festival in the good old Jewish way by sending money to Palestine to plant trees there, helping to make the land more beautiful and a better home for the Jews who have returned to Eretz Israel.

On the fourteenth day of the month of ADAR comes PURIM. Every Jewish child knows the story of this minor holiday so well that we will not stop to tell it here. Most of you, I am sure, have acted in plays telling the tale of the Jew-hating Haman, who was outwitted by beautiful Queen Esther and her uncle, the wise and faithful Mordecai. When King Ahasuerus ordered Haman's execution and then appointed

Mordecai as prime minister in his place, there was great rejoicing among the Jews, feasting and merrymaking, the exchange of presents and gifts to the poor. As Haman had cast lots (Purim) for a lucky day on which to kill his Jewish enemies, the name Purim, or Feast of Lots, has been given to the holiday.

But even if you have heard the story of the first Purim in faraway Persia, when Haman plotted against the Jews and Esther appeared unsummoned before the king to plead for her people, you may not know that we have had other Purims in our long and troubled history. One of the most interesting of these deliverances, which is still celebrated by many Oriental Jews, is the Purim of Saragossa, in which our old friend Elijah warned them against their enemy; another is kept at Algiers; another at Rhoades. In all of these tales of different times and places we find the same terrible danger to the Jewish people, the same miraculous deliverance.

Just now we want to hear how the only Purim we in America know is kept in the home and synagogue. Miriam and David and Joe, like Jewish children the world over, think it the jolliest of Jewish holidays. First of all there are presents from everybody to everybody in the family; even Dearie-Dear, the cross, old black tom-cat is remembered with a nice new red ribbon, which he always succeeds in scratching off before Purim is half over. There are presents of cakes and fruits and nuts and all sorts of things to relatives all over the city; these are packed in a pretty basket and covered with a white napkin.

"Because," as Miriam explains to Joseph, while she packs the SHALACH MONOTH, "everybody is supposed to provide Shalach Monoth on Purim. If a rich man carried an uncovered basket in the street, he might be too proud of his gift; and a poor man, who had to show that he wasn't giving much, would feel ashamed."

"But what does Shalach Monoth mean?" asked Joe.

"Send—money," answered David, very willing to show off his Hebrew. "I suppose people never send money presents any more to their friends. But when we dress up in our funny Purim clothes and go masking around to the neighbors, mother never scolds if they give us a few cents, though she wouldn't let us accept money any other time."

"That's because when she was a little girl they even were allowed to ask for it," explained Miriam. "Don't you know that little Yiddish song she told us she and her brothers used to sing when they went masquerading at Purim?

'Heut' is Purim; morgen is aus;
Giebt mir ein groschen und werf mich hinaus.'

Of course, they didn't expect to get thrown out, but they were sure of getting a penny.

"And, of course, we always give money to poor people on Purim just the way they did in the story of Esther," went on Miriam. "Father let David and me send some of our allowance to the orphan asylum last year. And he told us about the half shekel every Jew is supposed to give to the synagogue on Purim. Of course, we don't count our money by shekels any more, and a half shekel would only come to about ten cents in American money. But he said we ought to remember that a half shekel or a half of anything wasn't worth much until it was put with its other half. That's why Jews used to give it at Purim to remember to keep together and help one another out in times of danger."

Mother came into the room just then with another platter of cakes for the last baskets. Joseph promptly helped himself. "Why do you call 'em HAMANTASCHEN?" he asked.

THE FEAST OF PURIM
(*Moritz Oppenheimer*)

"The word means Haman's ears," answered mother, "because of the shape. And do you know why the rather bitter poppy seed is mixed with the sweet honey inside? To show that both good times and bad times fall to the Jew, but that he must always hope for help as he did in Queen Esther's day. The poppy seed is ground and pounded in that old brass pot over there which belonged to my grandmother. She told me once it was to teach us that no matter how the Jew is ground down by his enemies, he will still rise free and happy in the end. But now hurry up, you Shalach Monoth bringers, and take the baskets around. I want you home in time to go to synagogue and hear the Megillah read."

Hamantaschen

The MEGILLAH or Scroll of Esther is always read in the synagogue on the eve of Purim. The names of the wicked sons of the more wicked Haman are written one beneath the other; when they are read aloud every child who has been able to bring a Purim DREHER (rattle) shakes it as loudly as he can to drown the names. Another trick the boys enjoy is to write the names of these sons on their shoe soles; when the list is read off it is great fun to stamp as hard as possible as though on the treacherous Persians themselves.

Of course, most of this is in fun. We Jewish people no longer hate the scheming old Haman, dead so many hundreds of years. Although he was often used as an example of all the people who used the Jews cruelly, he was generally treated with good-natured contempt in the old Purim plays. The boy who played Haman usually acted not like a villain but a stupid clown; the rest of the actors took great pleasure in teasing him. These Purim plays were one of the brightest spots in the unhappy life of the ghetto Jew through the years of his persecution. He had no life outside the ghetto walls; in the ghetto his religion brought him real peace and happiness, but there was little uproarious gaiety except at Purim. Then everything was turned topsy-turvy. Grey-haired rabbis used to join in the merry Purim songs; boys and girls exchanged clothes and played pranks on each other; there was masking and the giving of Purim plays, followed by feasting. Today in America every religious school celebrates Purim with plays and parties; in Palestine the entire Jewish population takes part in the celebration, which because of its masking and noise-making can be compared to carnival times in some of our southern cities. The Seudah, a feast made up of all sorts of Purim dainties, is one of the jolliest features of this very jolly festival.

The day before Purim is observed as a fast day by many Jews in remembrance of the fast the Jews of Shushan kept with Esther before she went before the king. Also in memory of Esther a special Purim dish is served at the Seudah, consisting chiefly of cooked lentils. This is called BUB and represents the coarse meals Esther ate in the king's palace as she would taste no heathen food.

The fifteenth day of Adar is called SHUSHAN PURIM, as the Jews of the Persian city kept a second day of celebration and thanksgiving.

"That's a good idea," said David, thoughtfully. "I always have such a good time on Purim I wouldn't mind making it last two days if I could." And Miriam and Joe agreed with him.

SOMETHING TO ASK YOURSELVES

1. How many candles are burned to celebrate Chanukah? What is the Shammas and why did it receive its name?

2. Give the nature origin of other mid-winter festivals. The historical.

3. What is the meaning of the word Chanukah? Why is this festival also called the Feast of Lights? Why is it kept eight days?

4. Describe the trendel.

5. How are the Chanukah synagogue services distinguished from the usual service?

6. What is the meaning of Chamisha Asar? What kind of a holiday is it? How long has it been celebrated in Palestine? How is it celebrated in America today?

7. What is the meaning of Purim and why did the holiday receive its name?

8. How is Purim celebrated in the home?

9. How is Purim celebrated in the synagogue?

SOMETHING TO DO

1. If you are clever with your hands you might want to model a menorah out of clay. Even a very little boy like Joseph can do that. A big boy like David, who has studied manual training, should be able to construct a wooden menorah. Or what about a trendel? But be sure of your Hebrew lettering!

2. We've mentioned the Book of Judith in this chapter. It is a very interesting story. And you will want to read the story of the Maccabees for yourselves. The book of Judith and the two books of the Maccabees are called Apocrypha; you'll find out what this word means by looking it up in the dictionary or reading page 41 in *The Story of the Jew* (Levinger). Then get a copy of the Apocrypha from the Religious School library and read these exciting stories as they were written so long ago. If you haven't time—and children are so busy nowadays!—read the extract in the *Book of Jewish Thoughts* (page 257). This book was arranged by Dr. Hertz, and has many other fine bits about the Maccabean struggle.

3. The Chassidim (pious ones) refused to fight the Syrians on the Sabbath and were slain. Were the Maccabees right to break the Sabbath that they might save Judaism and the

Sabbath? This would make a good debate for class, or an essay for your religious school paper.

4. When you study Chamisha Asar, why don't you see how many allusions you can find to trees in your Bible? Find out how many of these trees grow in the United States.

5. Read a modern travel book on Palestine; then write a story on "How I celebrated Chamisha Asar in Palestine."

6. Here comes some more handwork—this time for Purim. Little boys like Joseph can cut out and decorate paper masks and make gold crowns for Queen Esther and King Ahasuerus to wear at the Purim party. Big boys like David may want to make something in manual training; say, Shalach Monoth for father or mother. (If you do, try to paint or carve a Magen David on it.) Or a Shalach Monoth box to collect pennies for your Purim charity. And in-between-girls, who are neither little nor big, like Miriam, will be sure to enjoy making some dresses for the Purim masquerade. You can make lovely ones out of crepe paper if you are careful; but I have better luck with any old thing I can find around the house, like kimonas or fancy bed spreads. (But you had better ask your mother before borrowing anything!) You might like to give a masquerade party at which you will wear them; ask everybody to come dressed like a character from Jewish history and see whether the guests can guess which each represents.

7. Prepare a Shalach Monoth basket for some shut-in; decorate it prettily and don't forget to cover it. If mother will help you make some Haman Taschen, all right; if not, it might be safer to put in something else.

8. Look up in the *Jewish Encyclopedia* (under Purim) the other Purims mentioned in this chapter. Describe the one you find the most interesting. (A good way is to pretend that you lived this thrilling experience yourself; describe it in a letter to a distant friend.)

SOMETHING TO READ

You have already been told about the Apocryphal books, Maccabees I and II, and Judith, which are interesting reading around Chanukah. For Purim you will want to read the Book of Esther, one of the most exciting stories you will ever find in the Bible or out of it. There are also a great many poems for the three festivals we have just studied together; you will find them in the collections of verses I have mentioned before. You will have your favorites, of course, but I want you to know mine: two Chanukah poems by our greatest American Jewish poet, Emma Lazarus, "The Banner of the Jew" and "Feast of Lights"; any of Jessie Sampter's charming verses on Chamisha Asar; and Helen Hunt's sonnet on Mordecai, the hero of Purim.

As for stories—well, here are a few of them:

For *Chanukah*: "Scars of Battle"; "The Severed Menorah," Rufus Learsi (*Kasriel the Watchman*); "A Hannukkah Night," Abram S. Isaacs (*The Young Champion*); "The Sacrifice at Modin," Emily Solis-Cohen (*David the Giant Killer*); "Candle Lights," Emily Goldsmith Gerson (*A Modern Esther*); "The Magic Top," Jehudah Steinberg (*Breakfast of the Birds*); "The Chanukah," Hannah Trager (*Festival Stories*); "What the Candles Say," A. S. Doniah (*Apples and Honey*). The following by Elma Ehrlich Levinger: "The Light that Never Failed" (*Jewish Holyday Stories*); "Friends" (*Playmates in Egypt*); "The Menorah of Remembrance" (*In Many Lands*); "In the Court of Antiochus"; "The Cruse of Oil"; "When the Lights Burned Low" (*Tales Old and New*).

Now for Chamisha Asar: "Iron and the Trees"; "Abraham's Tree," translated by Gerald Friedlander (*The Jewish Fairy Book*); "The Brave Little Olive Tree," which contains the story of Rabbi Choni and the Carob Tree, Elma Ehrlich Levinger (*Jewish Holyday Stories*); "The New Year of the Trees," translated by Elma Ehrlich Levinger (*Tales Old and New*).

And for Purim: "In Shushan the Capital," by Emily Solis-Cohen (*David the Giant Killer*); "A Modern Esther," Emily Goldsmith Gerson (*A Modern Esther*); "The Festival," Hannah Trager (*Festival Stories*); "Esther," Sholom Aleichem (*Jewish Children*); "How Esther Became Queen," Joseph Gaer (*The Magic Flight*). The following are by Elma Ehrlich

Levinger: "The Purim Pussy" (*Jewish Holyday Stories*) ; "The Purim Players" (*In Many Lands*) ; "The Sprig of Myrtle," (*Playmates in Egypt*) ; "The Cry of the Children"; "Purim and the Twins"; "A Disappointing Joke," (*Tales Old and New*).

X

SPRING FESTIVALS

The last few days before PASSOVER always seemed to Miriam to be the busiest days of the whole year. There was a visit to the dressmaker to fetch home the new dress she had been thinking about for weeks, for what is Passover without new clothes? Then little David had to be taken downtown for new shoes. He got restless on the car coming home and to quiet him Miriam told him her favorite Passover story, "Tish-cha-desh!" by the Hebrew writer Fischman. "Tish-cha-desh!" (New life to you!) is the old Jewish greeting to friends putting on a new garment. The story is of a poor tailor's son who every year before Passover delivered new clothes to his father's customers. The child never had owned a new suit, only cast-off clothing his father found time to cut down for him in his spare moments. No one had ever greeted him with Tish-cha-desh! not even at Passover, when the poorest Jew manages to buy some new bit of clothing for the spring festival. The little boy, ragged and hungry, worried so that he became ill. At last when he lay dying he saw lovely white angels flying about his bed; they carried a beautiful new suit of clothes and they sang Tish-cha-desh! Tish-cha-desh! as though welcoming him into heaven, where he might wear his fine new clothes forever and ever.

Miriam wiped her eyes at the end of the story, which little Joe thought rather foolish. "I don't see anything to cry about," he said, "as long as the boy got his clothes in time to wear them in heaven! I wonder if he got new shoes, too!"

and he looked proudly down at his new shiny brown ones with "big boy" thick soles and straps.

"I think boys are very hard-hearted and selfish," Miriam told him. "The next time you want a story you'd better go and read one in the funnies."

David was also busy, running to the Jewish grocery store for mother, to bring home horseradish and more eggs and big

 square boxes of MATZOS. And not only the family but the house had to be made ready to greet the Passover in a clean, fresh spring dress. Floors were scrubbed and clean curtains hung and rugs beaten; the Passover dishes, used only for this one week in the whole year, were taken down from the top shelf of the cupboard

Matzoth

and washed; the Passover silver was polished until it shone. Even mother got excited, and once when the telephone rang, just as she was dividing her time between tasting the home-made raisin wine and grating horse-radish, she actually shook her fist at the noisy instrument.

"I don't care who is calling up!" she declared. "I've got something else to do besides answering the telephone before PESACH!"

For once father had to help with the housework. According to the old custom it is the duty of the man of the family to search for leaven after the house has been made ready for the Passover. But let us begin at the beginning, as David says, and find out why there must be no leaven in the house for eight days.

Passover, as you heard in an earlier chapter, is one of the three great pilgrim feasts. It marks the passing of winter into spring and no doubt it began as a nature feast; the name, Pesach, comes from a Hebrew word meaning skip, or dance, and is thought to refer to the skipping of the young lambs. So in earliest times this was very likely a feast the shepherds kept before starting out to look for new pastures for their flocks. Later, when the wandering shepherds became farmers and settled in Palestine, offerings were taken to the Temple at Jerusalem. In the Book of Leviticus, the Israelites were commanded to bring as their offerings a lamb one year old without any blemish and a sheaf of grain from the first harvest, which falls earlier in the warm climate of Palestine than in this country.

But the historical beginnings of the Feast of the Passover are much more important. Passover falls on the tenth day of the first month of the Jewish calendar; NISAN was made the first month because it is the birth month of Israel as a nation. It marks the beginning of our history as a free people, for the name Passover suggests how the Jewish people, escaping from their Egyptian slavery, passed through the Red Sea, "from darkness into light, from slavery into freedom." The name also refers to the story of the Angel of Death, who slew the first-born of Egypt, but passed over the first-born of the Israelites, whose houses were marked with the blood of the newly sacrificed paschal lamb.

You all know the story of the Deliverance from Egypt; how Moses, after pleading in vain with Pharaoh to allow the children of Israel to go free, bade them sacrifice the paschal lamb and make ready for their long journey into the desert. We are told that in their haste to leave the land of bondage, where they had known such cruel hardships, the Israelites set out with dough still in their kneading troughs; this was later baked in the hot desert sun, forming thin flat cakes, much like the matzos we eat today during the Passover season. In memory of the flight from Egypt and the birth of Israel as a free nation, the descendants of these desert wanderers were commanded

THE SEDER ON PASSOVER EVE
(*Moritz Oppenheimer*)

to keep the Feast of the Unleavened Bread. Even to our day matzos are eaten for a whole week, which, when the festival is strictly observed, is ushered in by the Search after Leaven.

It is the leaven in bread and other foods which causes fermentation. None of this is to be allowed in the house during the eight days of Passover. So yesterday father passed from room to room in search of HOMETZ (leaven). When the last crumb was gathered he thanked God, who has given the commandment of removing the leaven, praying also that any bit which may have been overlooked be "destroyed and be like the dust of the earth."

But now it is time for the SEDER! Seder really means order (of the feast) or service; to Jewish children it has always meant the most wonderful Jewish holiday meal in the whole year. As soon as father returns from synagogue he takes his place at the head of the table; tonight his chair is heaped high with cushions to represent the couches once used at the festive meal. You know that in the olden days only free men were allowed to recline at meals while their slaves stood and served them. On this night of freedom the Jews, no matter how enslaved and ground down they were by their enemies, rested on cushions like free men, in remembrance of the freedom which had come to them on the first Passover. Beside father's place is an empty chair for Elijah, whom we expect to visit every Seder table; for it is Elijah the Friend who will usher in the Messiah to free Israel. So what better time to expect him than on Israel's Night of Freedom? The large goblet of wine on the table is also reserved for Elijah.

The larger platter before father bears the various symbols of the feast. First, the folded napkin with three matzos placed one between each fold, each piece of unleavened bread representing a division of the Jewish people, Cohen, Levi, and Israelite. The lamb bone represents the sacrificial lamb; the roasted egg is a symbol of hope and resurrection; from the seemingly dead egg comes life, from winter spring, from slavery freedom. The parsley and the horseradish root are the greens typifying spring; later the parsley is dipped into salt water (tears shed in slavery) and the bitter horseradish root eaten with sweet HAROSETH (a mixture of apples and nuts and wine) which by its red color suggests the bricks made during Egyptian slavery. Life holds both bitter and sweet, as Jews must have remembered at their Passover feasts year after year, often in lands where they were hated and hunted and put to death for their religion. Yet they never lost courage, and every Passover festival ended with the old hope: We celebrate Passover this year in the land of exile; but next year we will spend it in Jerusalem.

One of the most important parts of the Seder is the Four Questions asked by the youngest child, who inquires concerning the meaning of the feast. Little Joseph was very proud of being allowed to ask them this year; his uncle answered him and explained the meaning of the symbols on the Seder dish. Another feature of the service, which is meant to keep the children interested during the long evening of prayers and explanations, is the hiding of the matzos. Part of the middle matzo is kept for the AFIKOMAN (dessert); part is hidden and the child finding it may expect a present. Later you will see what Miriam's present was. But perhaps the children like best of all CHAD GADYAH, the story written in Aramaic and sung to an old melody, which tells of the Kid (Israel) that my Father (God) bought for two pieces of money (the two tablets on which the Ten Commandments were written). It is one of the world's oldest nursery rhymes, like the House that Jack Built. But it also has a deep religious meaning, and every figure in it represents a great event in the long, wonderful history of the Jewish people. A child is usually asked to open the door during the service, to invite the stranger who may be passing to come in. This custom may go back to the days when the Jews were accused of using human blood at their festival and wanted to show that they had nothing to conceal from their neighbors.

Like Succoth, the first two and the last two days of the festival are observed. The Song of Songs is read during the synagogue service; as a story of spring in Palestine it is appropriate for a springtide holyday. Because it tells the love story of a beautiful shepherdess and contains several marriage songs, it also reminds us of God's love for Israel whom He led out of Egypt.

Miriam's gift for finding the Afikoman was a bow and arrows. Of course, she had to let the boys use them on LAG BA'OMER. This holiday is also a nature as well as a historical festival. After the service on the eve of the second day of Passover the counting of the Omer begins. An Omer (which here is used to mean harvest) is a measure about the size of half a gallon; it contained some of the wheat of the first harvest, which was brought as an offering for the priests at Jerusalem. This counting lasts for seven weeks. The days of counting, which are called the SEFIRAH days, are a time of unhappy memories for the Jews, because at this period there were terrible massacres, under the Roman emperors and later during the Crusades. Neither marriages nor feasts may take place during the Sephira days, with the exception of the New Moon and the thirty-third day of the Omer, which is known as Lag Ba'omer.

Lag Ba'omer, which is also known as the Scholar's Holiday, is a time of rejoicing; for on that day, we are told, the prayers of the pupils of the gentle sage, Rabbi Akiba, brought about the end of a terrible plague in Palestine. In Europe,

Jewish boys were allowed to leave their books and roam about the fields, that they might remember how once the Jewish people had broad lands of their own. They were told the legend of Rabbi Simeon ben Yohai who remained hidden in a cave during the persecutions of the Romans for fourteen years. When he died, the rainbow, which had not been seen for many years, appeared in the sky to remind the Jews of his prophecy that before the Messiah came to free the Jewish people, they should see a bow of many colors in the sky. So in his memory, these Jewish school boys carried bows and arrows as they roamed the woods and fields and wondered when the Jewish nation would again come to its own land.

Miriam's Hebrew School gave a Lag Ba'omer party. There were refreshments, of course, and a play about Rabbi Akiba and Bar Kochba, the last of the Jewish warriors against Rome. Afterwards the children had an archery contest. Miriam always insisted that she won the prize because she had been practising since after Passover with the bow and arrows her father had given her for finding the Afikoman!

After the fifty days, or seven weeks, of counting the Omer comes SHABUOTH, the Feast of Weeks. Shabuoth is chiefly a festival of the synagogue where special services are held for two days. But in the home it is sometimes celebrated by serving dairy foods, as milk is especially plentiful in Palestine at that season of the year. Honey is also eaten to remind us of the sweetness of the Torah given to Israel on that day. (When did we see this custom before?) At one time a Sinai cake was served, made to represent a ladder with seven rungs for the seven spheres through which God passed when He descended to give the Law to Moses. This day was especially interesting to school children in the Middle Ages as many of them were taken to the Hebrew school for the first time on Shabuoth. For, says the old story, when God wanted a pledge that Israel would always keep His commandments, Moses promised that the little children would be true to the Law, and it was bestowed upon the people.

"Shabuoth," as father explained to the children, "is one of the three great pilgrim feasts like Passover and Succoth. It is sometimes called the Festival of the First Fruits, because after the counting of the Omer an offering of first fruits was brought to the Temple at Jerusalem. This offering was arranged in a special way, with barley at the bottom of the basket and wheat above; over the wheat they placed olives, then dates and finally figs; this was beautifully decorated with leaves. Another offering was the twin loaves made out of the new grain. Later when there was no Temple to which to bring offerings, the Jews decorated their synagogues with flowers and spread fresh grass upon the floor to celebrate the Giving of the Law."

"Then Shabuoth is another farmer, or nature, holiday," said Miriam.

"Yes. But the historical part is the most important. Most people believe that Shabuoth is the greatest day in the national history of Israel. On Passover the people became a free nation, but on Shabuoth they received the Ten Commandments. Now instead of being a little desert tribe they became the nation that was to influence all mankind. For all civilized men today base their laws on those commandments which the Children of Israel received as they stood at the foot of Mount Sinai.

"You know the story of Ruth, children," continued father. "How she was a stranger from the strange land of Moab and came to Israel with her dead husband's mother, Naomi. She was not only a good daughter to Naomi; she accepted the religion of Israel and obeyed it faithfully. Because Ruth was so loyal to the Law, her story in the Book of Ruth is read in the synagogue services at Shabuoth. There is also a legend that King David was born and died on Shabuoth; so it is appropriate to read Ruth's story at this time as she was given the honor of becoming the ancestress of this most loved of Jewish kings."

Israel Zangwill has translated from the Hebrew a poem telling how Moses was permitted

To Fetch the Torah Down

The Angels came a-mustering,
A-mustering, a-mustering,
The Angels came a-clustering
Around the sapphire throne.
A-questioning of one another,
Of one another, of one another,
A-questioning each one his brother
Around the sapphire throne.
Pray who is he, and where is he,
And where is he, and where is he,
Who shining casts—so fair is he—
A shadow on the throne?
Pray who has up to heaven come,
To heaven come, to heaven come,
Through all the circles seven come,
To fetch the Torah down?
'Tis Moses up to heaven come,
To heaven come, to heaven come,
Through all the circles seven come,
To fetch the Torah down.

Now that we have gone around the Jewish year and enjoyed the Jewish festivals, we want to stop for a moment to learn about the Jewish fast days. We have already read of Yom Kippur, the great White Fast, and mentioned the Fast of Esther, which comes just before Purim. There are other fast days scattered through the year, and kept as a sign of mourning for great griefs which have come to the Jewish people,

such as the tenth of TEBET (December), the day on which began the siege of Jerusalem by Nebuchadnezzar; the seventeenth
of TAMMUZ (July) in remembrance of the breach made in the
city wall; and the third day of TISHRI (September), in memory
of the noble Gedalia, who was murdered during his attempt
to resettle the land laid waste by the armies of Babylon.

The FEAST OF TAMMUZ begins the three weeks of mourning
for the destruction of the Temple. During this time luxuries
like meat and certain amusements are forbidden. The last
nine days (from the first to the ninth of AB, usually August)
are kept even more strictly. The last day, the NINTH OF AB,
which marks the destruction of both the First and Second
Temples, is the saddest day in the whole Jewish calendar.

Kept as a fast day from the eve of the Ninth of Ab to sunset of the following day, it is spent in the synagogue in remembrance of the past glories of Israel. Candles are often burned
as in memory of the dead while the congregation sit upon the
floor like mourners. The lamentations of Jeremiah are read,
for Jeremiah, the sorrowful prophet, is believed to have seen
the destruction of Jerusalem. As he viewed the charred and
still burning walls of the Temple and watched the unhappy
Jews, bound in chains, driven down the road toward Babylon,
Jeremiah began his beautiful and touching poem on his ruined
home: "How doth the city sit solitary, which was full of
people." Yet even in these sad verses Jeremiah dares hope
that some day God will comfort Zion.

Centuries later, the Second Temple was destroyed by the
Roman soldiers on the Ninth of Ab. So this day became a
memorial for the two blackest tragedies in Jewish history.

One wall remained in the place where once the Temple
stood in high Jerusalem. It is called the WAILING WALL; here
for centuries faithful Jews from all over the world have come
to weep over the woes of Israel. But a new day has now dawned

for the scattered, long-wandering people. In earlier chapters we have read how the Children of Israel, returning to the Mother Land, are toiling to make barren places blossoming and fruitful once more. I have tried to picture this in one of my poems; here is the last stanza of

O LITTLE LAND OF LONG AGO

O little land of long ago,
   Beneath the smiling skies,
Where old men weep for Judah's woe
   A holier shrine shall rise.
Our sons will build Jerusalem
   In sweat and blood and pain:
Rejoice, rejoice, O little land,
   For we come home again!

SOMETHING TO ASK YOURSELF

1. What are the preparations for Passover?
2. Describe Passover as a nature festival.
3. When does Passover fall? Why is it such an important historical holiday?
4. Why is Passover called the Feast of the Unleavened Bread? How long does it last?
5. What does the word Seder mean? Why are there cushions in father's chair? Why is Elijah connected with Passover?
6. Describe the things found on the Seder plate and give the meaning of each symbol.
7. What parts do children take in the Seder?
8. What Bible book is read in the synagogue during Passover services and why?
9. What is the meaning of Lag Ba'omer? Give the names of three great Jews always remembered at this festival and tell what you know about them.
10. What is the meaning of Shabuoth?
11. Why were children brought to the Hebrew school for

the first time on Shabuoth, and why is the modern rite of confirmation celebrated on this holyday?

12. Why is the story of Ruth read in the synagogue at Shabuoth?

13. Name the Jewish fast days you know and tell what event in Jewish history each recalls.

14. What portion of the Bible is read on Tisha B'ab and why?

Something to Do

1. Write a little play in which one scene shows either: a group of Jews going up to Jerusalem to keep the Passover in the days when the Temple stood; or, a modern family seated about the Seder table; or, a little child waits for Elijah to visit his home on Seder night.

2. If you are a girl (don't be impatient, boys, your turn is coming next!) prepare a Passover cook book for a young Jewish housekeeper. Get the recipes for Passover dainties from your mother or look them up in some Jewish cook book. Paste them in a folder decorated with pictures you may either draw or cut from magazines. An interesting design would be pictures of the symbols of the Passover—a big wine glass, an egg and so on. Or the figures of the characters mentioned in the Chad Gadyah.

3. Which reminds me! Look up in any Haggadah (book with the services of the Seder in it) the story of Chad Gadyah and tell the class the meaning of the Kid and the people and animals which tried to kill it.

4. Now, boys, if you want to, why don't you try to make bows and arrows for Lag Ba'omer and have a real Lag Ba'omer archery party? If the girls behave, let them come, too. Especially if they promise to bring the refreshments!

5. Dramatize the story of Ruth in class. Everybody who is going to take part must read the story as it is so beautifully told in the Bible. Then give out the parts and act out the adventures of Ruth and Naomi. If the class like it, several of you might want to write it down, polish the play a little, fix up costumes and give it for the whole school at assembly.

6. I have seen book ends with a picture of the tablets of

the Law carved on each end. Boys who have had manual training would like to do this; you could carve a Magen David
at the top.

SOMETHING TO READ

As usual, there are plenty of poems about these holy days
in the books I have listed before. And you will surely want to
read all of the Book of Ruth and at least a chapter of Lamentations and the Song of Songs.

For *Passover* I have found a great many stories; I think you
will like any of the following: "Prince Tothan and Tamarah"
and "The First Plague," Joseph Gaer (*The Magic Flight*);
"Two Elijahs," Rufus Learsi, (*Kasriel the Watchman*); "The
Luck of the Cohens" and "Home Again," Emily Goldsmith
Gerson, (*A Modern Esther*); "A Tale of the Passover," Hannah Trager, (*Festival Stories*); "The Breakfast of the Birds,"
Jehudah Steinberg, (*Breakfast of the Birds*); "Elijah's Goblet," Israel Zangwill, (*Ghetto Comedies*); "Elijah the Prophet," Sholom Aleichem, (*Apples and Honey*, a book of stories
and poems by different Jewish authors, you will be sure to
enjoy); "The Passover Guest," Sholom Aleichem, (*Yiddish
Tales*); "How Shimmele Became a Sceptic," Martha Wolfenstein, (*Idylls of the Gass*). In my own books you will find
the following: "A Real Passover," (*Jewish Holyday Stories*);
"Playmates in Egypt," (*Playmates in Egypt*); "The Unwel-
come Guest," (*In Many Lands*); "A Spring Song," "The Best-
Ever Seder," "A Son of Egypt," "The Lamb of Sacrifice," "The
Passover Stranger," (*Tales Old and New*).

For *Lag Ba'omer*: "The Goblin and the Princess," Gerald
Friedlander, (*Jewish Fairy Book*); "The Spoiled Holiday,"
Jehudah Steinberg, (*The Breakfast of the Birds*); "A Lost
Lag Ba'omer," Sholom Aleichem, (*Jewish Children*); "Lag
Ba'omer," Hannah Trager, (*Festival Stories*); "Roamers in the
Night," Rufus Learsi, (*Kasriel the Watchman*); "Why are
Cherries Red," Joseph Gaer, (*The Magic Flight*); "When
Giants Roamed Palestine" and "Stories Told by the Rabbis,"
Max Weis, (*Great Men in Israel*). By Elma Ehrlich Levinger:
"The Bow that Would Not Bend," (*Jewish Holyday Stories*);
"Akiba, the Peaceful Soldier," "Bar Kochba, the Son of a

Star," (*Great Jews Since Bible Times*); "The Long Night," "The Dove and the Eagle," (*In Many Lands*); "The Joy of Weeping," (*Tales Old and New*); "Akiba," by Marcus Lehmann.

For *Shabuoth*: "When the Skies Open at Midnight," Joseph Gaer, (*The Magic Flight*); "The Seven Little Men," Rufus Learsi, (*Kasriel the Watchman*); "Pentecost or the Pilgrimage," Hannah Trager, (*Festival Stories*); "Greens for Shabuoth," Sholom Aleichem, (*Jewish Children*); "The Lesson of the Harvest," Abram S. Isaacs (*Stories of the Rabbis*); "Amid the Alien Corn," Emily Solis-Cohen, (*David the Giant Killer*). Elma Ehrlich Levinger: "The Lad Who Brought no Offering," (*Playmates in Israel*); "Clothes," (*Jewish Holyday Stories*); "A Rose for Beauty," (*In Many Lands*); "The Boy Who Could Sing," "The White Flower," (*Tales Old and New*).

For *Tisha B'ab*: "The Sword of the Spirit," Rufus Learsi, (*Kasriel the Watchman*); "The Swallow," "Service," "The Last Farthing," Jehudah Steinberg, (*Breakfast of the Birds*). By Elma Ehrlich Levinger: "The Temple Wall," "The Sleeping Beauty," (*Tales Old and New*); "The Vision that Passed," (*In Many Lands*); "The Western Wall," (*Jewish Holyday Stories*).

XI

A GOOD-BYE CHAPTER—AND A SHORT ONE!

To the boys and girls who have read thus far: We have spent some hours together in the Jewish home and the synagogue, and now it is time to say good-bye. When Jews meet they often repeat the old Hebrew greeting, SHALOM! (peace); when the priest blessed the departing people, he prayed to God to keep them and give them peace. So Shalom! to you, my readers, every one of you!

Perhaps you have not seen many of the ceremonies described in this book; perhaps you will never care to practise them. I do not know. But I do know that there is great happiness in being a Jew. To me, to be a Jew means to know and love the beautiful customs of the fathers and to keep as many of them as you can; to be one of the congregation of Israel; to love and upbuild Palestine, the ancient homeland.

Most of you are still very young and do not see the importance of many of the things we have discussed together in these pages. But some day you will be older; some of you will be leaders in the synagogue; many of you will have homes of your own. And if you try, you can make both the synagogue and the Jewish home two of the most beautiful places on earth because of the love for Judaism which you carry in your hearts.

APPENDIX

(Which means something added on that children never bother to read; but I hope the teachers will!)

REFERENCE BOOKS FOR TEACHERS

Teachers will find the following works most valuable not only for reference, but for building up a background for the material studied in this book:

Jewish Encyclopedia.
Judaism as Creed and Life, Morris Joseph.
Services in Synagogue and Home, Lewis N. Dembitz.
Jewish Ceremonial Institutions and Customs, William Rosenau.
The Jewish Religion, Julius H. Greenstone.
The Jewish Religion, H. Pereira Mendes.
The Jewish Library, edited by Leo Jung.
The Three Pillars, Deborah Melamed.
Legends of the Jews, Ginzberg.
The Jewish Anthology, Edmund Fleg.
Jewish Life in the Middle Ages, Israel Abrahams.
Festival Studies, Israel Abrahams.
The Project Method in the Jewish School, Emanuel Gamoran.

CLASS PROJECTS

This subject has been hardly more than touched upon in the preceding pages. Any wide-awake teacher will think of a dozen more as she reads each chapter. One project especially may be spread over a year's work and cannot be left to the pupils: a Ceremonial Exhibition. This may be given either as an independent class project or in connection with the Sisterhood. Ceremonial objects may be brought to class from month to month as they are studied; at the end of the year they should all be brought back to be exhibited at a religious school meeting.

123

*WITH

THE

JEWISH CHILD*

Pupils should be assigned to prepare talks upon the various objects, giving as much background material as possible, not only the stories and poems found in this book, but others from the above references. Several members of the class may want to give an original play written during the year and based on the ceremonials studied or the dramatization of a poem like Zangwill's "The Hebrew's Friday Night." Such an exhibition would not only serve as a review of the year's work, but would vivify text book lessons. If desired there might be two exhibitions—one after the first section of the book is completed, devoted to the ceremonies of the home and synagogue; the second descriptive of the ceremonies of the holydays.

ACKNOWLEDGEMENTS

In a few cases, for the sake of simplicity, the name of the translator of a poem was not included. The names which were omitted in the text are:

Abraham Burstein ...."The Angel's Gift"
Abraham Burstein ...."The Angel's Gift"
Margaret Armour ...."Princess Sabbath"
Mrs. Henry Lucas ...."Yigdal"
Samuel S. Grossman ...."New Year of the Trees"